Silent Separations

SUBHASH PURI

SILENT SEPARATIONS

Broken Hearts in Unbroken
Relationships

BookSurge Publishing
2006

Edited by Rachna Vohra (www.sapostrophe.org)

Copyright © 2006 Subhash Puri
All rights reserved.
ISBN: 1-4196-5197-8
Library of Congress Control Number: 2006909482

To order additional copies, please contact us.
BookSurge, LLC
www.booksurge.com
1-866-308-6235
orders@booksurge.com
Books can also be ordered from:
www.Amazon.com

Silent Separations

To Our Children And Grand Children …
Naven, Pamela
And Jaden And Jared
Mark, Anu
And Annika

If We Are The Cause Of Your Existence,
You Are The Purpose Of Our Life.
Our Fondest Love.

This book is not about you or me;
It is about the "distance" between us.
The Silent Separations

CONTENTS

Prologue: The Writer on his Writings   xiii

Section 1: Panorama – The New Vision   1
Chapter 1: Introduction: A New Paradigm for Relationships
Chapter 2: Silent Separations   15

Section 2: Ground Zero – The Understanding
Chapter 3: Relationships: A Reality Check   25
Chapter 4: The Makings and Breakings of Relationships   31
Chapter 5: The Process of Life   55

Section 3: Journey into the Unknown – The Reason
Chapter 6: The Person – The Personality – The Persona   63
Chapter 7: Silent Stress   67
Chapter 8: Mental Tape   71
Chapter 9: Variety   79
Chapter 10: Righteousness   87
Chapter 11: Ego   93
Chapter 12: Aggressiveness   107
Chapter 13: Maturity   117
Chapter 14: Thinking   123
Chapter 15: Anger   129
Chapter 16: Fantasy   137
Chapter 17: Expectations   143
Chapter 18: Fulfillment   149

Section 4: Quantum Leap – The Awakening
Chapter 19: Awakenings and Inner-Evolution   157
Chapter 20: The Story of Adam and Eve   161
Chapter 21: The Dilemma   177

Section 5: Final Frontiers – The Resolve

Chapter 22: Break the Silence   183

Chapter 23: Empty the Tape   187

Chapter 24: Control the Righteousness Syndrome   191

Chapter 25: Drop the Ego   195

Chapter 26: Tame the Aggressiveness   201

Chapter 27: The New Reconciliation   205

Chapter 28: Humble Surrenders   211

Chapter 29: Pearls of Wisdom – The Lessons Learnt   217

The Epilogue

A Bouquet of Roses for My Children   235

PROLOGUE
THE WRITER ON HIS WRITINGS

"Love is not a happening;
It's a realization."

With a consuming passion for understanding the intricacies of human nature, the first and most intriguing facet that caught my attention, was "human relationships". When I looked around, I found that this is one domain of human life and living that is suffering the most. It was quite disturbing to see the ever-growing problem of relationship disharmony and disintegration, with a continued deterioration of our relationships. It takes us longer to make a relationship than to break it. We are constantly wrapped up in the unending cycle of "– makings – breakings – re-makings – re-breakings – ..." of relationships. And this is despite the fact that relationships are an inherent necessity of life – we just cannot live without them. Even more disturbing was the fact that despite the importance of relationships to life, this is one subject that is never taught to us, formally or informally, throughout our upbringing, or in our entire life for that matter. We learn everything else in life – science, arts, medicine, music, etc. – but not the subject most needed for human life – "relationships". It is one subject that each of us learns on our own, simply as a by-product of growing up, and we surely do a pretty lousy job.

Two very significant, but disturbing questions that came out of my deep contemplation and observations were:

- Why do our relationships go bad and break, especially when we know that relationships are almost an integral part of life. They are a compulsive necessity of life and living, and we have to have them.

- And more importantly, why are we incapable of reconciling our relationships more on a permanent basis? Why are we still wrapped up in the unending cycle of "makings – breakings" of relationships, despite our best efforts and intentions?

That was it – that was the light at the end of the tunnel that I was looking for – a purpose manifested itself – a passion was born. Or in my particular case, the passion was re-ignited – the passion to study "human relationships". This book is the result of that life-long passion.

What is passion?

Passion is a reinforcement of a desire. Passion is desire with a determination. Being feeling and thinking machines, as we humans basically are, desires and passions are a profoundly important and integral part of our lives. To achieve something extraordinarily unique for which you have a consuming passion, your basic professional knowledge, understanding, and experience is, of course, very essential, but is not enough – you have to have a deep zest and compelling passion for it.

I am sure that everybody has a passion for something, or perhaps everybody has to have a passion for something – for passion is the energy and force that drives our life. Passion is the dynamism of life. I have a passion too, and my passion, which is ready to go into action, is to study the dilemma of relationship disharmony.

After considerable time and patience, focussed research and experiential observations, I was able to find the missing link in our understanding. I came to a simple, but painful, conclusion: that the fundamental reason as to why we are unable to resolve the dilemma of relationships is because our present understanding of why relationships fail and how to reconcile them is seriously deficient and inadequate. Now, if you say that this is not true, or that it is not the case, then tell me why are we still grappling with the issue, despite our overwhelming knowledge about the subject?

As we go along in the book, I shall systematically present my new thoughts and visions to elaborate the subject. The perspectives and paradigms that I am presenting are simple and are a matter of commonsense reality of everyday life and living. Yet, they do present some radically new perspectives on relationships that have never before been explored or discussed, at least in the schema in which I am presenting them.

Before we go any deeper into the subject, I must forewarn you that the subject of relationships is a highly emotionally charged and mature subject. And as such, it requires you to generate, as a minimum, a genuine interest, a keen sense of observation, ability for deep introspective thinking, a profound thought maturity, and last but not least, true empathy for the human person. Also, because the subject is very attention demanding, you also need to generate a pleasant and palatable frame of mind and a good reading mindset.

Writing a book on the emotional aspects of human nature is, by no means, an easy task. It is as difficult for the writer to write, as it is for the reader to read and comprehend. Every book has a tinge of its author's personal life experiences and emotions – to a greater or lesser degree – depending on the nature of the subject matter. But books relating to human feelings and emotions are virtually brimming with the author's own emotions and experiences. You just cannot simply concoct, out of your mind, a subject as sensitive as human emotions and behavior – you really have to live through it to understand and feel in order to be able to express it with full emotional integrity. As such, therefore, this book is no exception – it is the result of almost a whole life of deep introspective and retrospective thinking, observations, and research. It is the result of a personal passion – a passion to understand why we behave the way we do, and how our behavior influences the makings and breakings of our relationships. To that extent, the book can be appropriately considered as an autobiography of relationships, or a collective biography of us all.

Finally, there is the matter of logistics about my writings that I must clarify right here. This book is written – almost totally – in the communicative style, as if I am speaking to you directly – one-on-one. The book is free from any strict regimentations of grammar or perfect sentence structuring. My aim is to present a free flow of my unique thoughts, ideas, and feelings in the way that I feel comfortable and in the language in which we speak with each other on a daily basis. And, if you can clearly understand what I am saying, then we have both accomplished our task. The book is simply an unending flow of thoughts from the stream of my consciousness, and the stream of consciousness doesn't recognize any commas, periods, punctuations, or grammar. Additionally, I must warn you that I may be introducing many new words and phrases that don't even exist in the dictionary – so please don't bother looking them up, though I promise you they will be totally understandable.

Last but not least – the important task of saying "thanks".

Life is nothing more than an interplay of relationships of one kind or another. It is a platform on which we all collectively live, learn, and grow.

Our understanding and wisdom is obviously, therefore, a by-product of our mutual interactions. The same holds true for the process of learning about the makings and breakings of relationships. No author can be so boastful and presumptuous as to believe that something utterly original can be created in isolation. It is always through uninhibited interactions and the influence of writings and conversations with friends and relatives that a person gains an experiential insight and wisdom into the subject.

I would, therefore, like to pay my tribute of profound gratitude to all with whom I have interacted and associated in any form of relationship – for it is through those associations that I have learned what I know today.

My special thanks go to my friends and relatives who have sought my help and guidance in understanding, resolving, and enriching their relationships and lives – for the process of mentoring, in turn, gave me more and more maturity of thought and understanding, thus enriching my own life and wisdom.

SECTION 1
PANORAMA
THE NEW VISION

1

INTRODUCTION:
A NEW PARADIGM FOR RELATIONSHIPS

"Knowledge is not wisdom;
Knowledge comes from the outside;
Wisdom comes from within."

This book presents a new and unique perspective for the ever-growing problem of relationship disharmony and disintegration. Just so that you can appreciate, more discriminatingly, the uniqueness of the new thoughts and ideas presented in this book, I thought it may be more useful to provide you with a panoramic view of the basic framework of my ideas, right up front in this introductory chapter. I believe that this would help generate a favourable mindset that will facilitate the comprehension of these rather sensitive but challenging thoughts in a more lucid and intelligible manner. Indeed, the highlights are only meant to give you an overall directional schema – you may still have to tread the path slowly and systematically – for the subject of relationships is a highly emotionally charged and mature issue, and it requires the full span of your attention. A more detailed treatment of the subject will begin in section 2.

How was the new idea conceived, why was it needed, and how is my perspective better and more unique from our current understanding of the problem of relationship breakdowns? The answer to the first question is rather obvious. Much like the conception and development of any other project, this one had the same four ingredients: a serious and disturbing issue provoked a thought; a strong desire was born to do something about it; a deep introspective and retrospective bout of experiential observations and research went into action; and finally, the passion kept pushing the determination until a new and viable solution emerged. Actually, in my particular case, there was no provocation needed, because my life is already replete with a deep passion for the study of human nature and relationships. And the current state of deteriorating health of the "relationship union" simply added more fuel to the passion.

Human relationships!!! They surely are in a mess — spoken or unspoken — silent or vocal — and we all know it. We can all see it, feel it, and smell it in the air — it's all around us. There is a deep sense of prevailing disharmony and unhappiness in our relationships — and it's neither a secret nor a private joke.

Brother is sore with the brother; mother-in-laws are constantly at odds with daughter-in-laws; spouses constantly pick on each other on every issue; friends are angry with friends; the son doesn't want to listen to the father; … ; the list is endless, and the domain incessantly wide. And, this is despite the indomitable fact that relationships are an essential and irrevocable part of life and living — we cannot live without them. Relationships are the lifeline to life.

It somehow seems as if we are constantly uptight, super-sensitive, and at odds with each other. A meaninglessly trivial behavioral mistake or misunderstanding can hurt our false ego-pride and throw us off-balance. Why is it so? Why do we constantly fight and bicker with each other? Why can't we live peacefully in relationships, especially when we know that we have to? These are the questions, which led me to my journey.

The Big Question

The two obvious questions that arose out of this observational dilemma were:

1. Why do our relationships go bad or break?
2. Why do our reconciliation efforts fail to provide permanent relationship harmony? Why are we constantly wrapped up in the unending cycle of "makings — breakings — re-makings — re-breakings …" of relationships?

Although these two are the most fundamental questions about the relationship dilemma, there is another very perplexing issue: Why is our current system unable to answer these questions appropriately, and why are we incapable of bringing in a permanent sense of reconciliation in the relationship? Is it really that intractable an issue, or is it that there is some gap or deficiency in our current understanding of the "real" nature of relationship harmony. For, as I asked myself — we have so much accumulated knowledge of the subject – so many books have been written on the dilemma, we are still without answers. Also, the subject has been so fiercely debated, over and over again, by all levels of scholars, professionals, and practitioners – why haven't they been able to develop a workable solution so far?

It was then that I decided to undertake this formidable task of studying the problem to see if it is the weaknesses of our current thinking, or if it is something else that is not allowing us to adequately resolve this dilemma of "makings and breakings" of relationships. After a considerable expenditure of time and patience and systematic experiential observations and research, I was able to see some light at the end of the tunnel. I was able to break the code and decipher the dilemma of that "why" – why do our relationships break? A new and very unique vision ultimately manifested itself – a new paradigm was born. I came to a very simple, but powerful, conclusion that:

- Our present understanding of why and how relationships go bad is inadequate and deficient.
- Our current reconciliation methods and strategies are weak and inappropriate.

It was, of course, a daringly difficult task to challenge the entire existing framework of our understanding, of our literature, and of our current practices of counselling and psychotherapy, on which we have come to rely for so long, and which we have so extensively utilized to resolve our relationship problems. But somehow, it was not too difficult for me to come up with that conclusion, for, as I said to myself – and perhaps, I may even ask you also – if our current understanding is correct and complete, then why are we still grappling with the issue? Why are we still unable to break out of that unending cycle of "makings and breakings" despite our best efforts and intentions, and despite the overwhelming help of our mentors?

The Missing Link

Although the main focus of my research was to find answers to those two big questions about failing relationships, yet my research process identified and highlighted some additional serious deficiencies in our current system with regards to the extent of the relationship domain. Basically, the following four new shortcomings of the current system were identified by my research:

1. Magnitude: That our estimate of the extent and magnitude of the problem is incomplete.

2. Dimension: That our current focus on the dimensions of different types of relationships is very narrow and inadequate.

3. Breakings: That our present understanding of how and why relationships go bad is incomplete and deficient.

4. Re-Makings: That our present approach to reconciliation is quite weak and inadequate.

Put together, these four shortcomings collectively turned out to be the main causes of our inability to understand and ameliorate the issue appropriately. The first two findings relate, mostly, to the logistics of the relationship domain, that is, to the extent of the problem; and the last two pertain to the main issue, that of makings and breakings of relationships. We shall now examine them one by one.

Although these revelations are very bold and challenging, without them we would still be grappling with the issue for a long time to come. To find more befitting models, better than the ones we already have, we unfortunately have to challenge and shake up the basic foundation of our current modus operandi, and we cannot afford to let arrogance and complacency block our way.

The Expanded Relationship Field

The first paradigm – that of "magnitude" – pertains to the extent of the problem. Our current preoccupation, as you can see, is primarily focused only on the aspects of separations and/or divorces for the marital-type of relationships. This preoccupation is obvious because all of our literature, media, and all of our statistics are focused on only this facet of relationships. In doing so, unfortunately, we have ignored a much larger group whose relationship problems are as, or more, painful than the marital group. This group consists of those people who are still living together in relationships, even when they are hopelessly unhappy. They don't want to break the relationship for one reason or another, and at the same time they don't want to live into it either. I call them the "silent separation" – "lonesome togetherness" category. If you look around your own circle of relationships, you would be absolutely amazed to find how big this category is – with many couples still living together, but unhappily. And this category is wildly outstretched across all borders and boundaries. Surprisingly, nobody has ever written about or discussed them – even when knowledge about this group can profoundly enhance our understanding of why marital relationships fail. This revelation was so significant for me that I even decided to name the book by that title – "Silent Separations – Broken Hearts in Unbroken Relationships".

The second revelation – that of "dimension" – points to the fact that we have also downplayed the role of the relationship of "relatives", even when we know that, most often the core marital relationship suffers its demise because of unwanted interference by relatives in the interplay of the couple. Consequently, the study of the relationship of relatives is of paramount importance to understanding and resolving problems relating to marital relationships. With these two revelations, we would now be dealing with an "expanded relationship field" – one that encompasses all types of relationships.

Breakings/Re-Makings: The Core Paradigms

Let us now consider the other two aspects – the main paradigms for "breakings" and "reconciliations" – where I feel there is a serious gap in our current understanding and practices. To highlight and accentuate the uniqueness of my new paradigms, so that you can appreciate what new I am presenting, I shall first present the framework of our current understanding, and then follow it up with the framework of my new perspectives.

Our Present Perspective

The Breakings: Why do relationships break? As a matter of commonsense understanding, our relationships suffer their ups and downs and go bad because of our bad behavior and actions – that is, what we say to each other and how we behave with each other. In the course of our day-to-day interactions and confrontations, we react to each other in a certain way. If the nature and content of that reaction is not to our liking, or is not commensurate with the way we think and perceive things, we get annoyed and unhappy, and consequently, a feeling of anger and antagonism sets in. Now, if you multiply this single interactive scenario a hundred-fold, and extend it over a period of time, you can see that a cumulative antagonistic mindset is generated. This cumulative build-up is what I annotate as the "mental tape" effect – a phenomenon that I shall elucidate in a subsequent chapter. The mental tape is a storehouse of our impressions about others "as we see them", and this becomes the basis of how we interact and react with each other and how we maintain or break the relationship. The tape gets filled up with antagonistic feelings as we go along, and when it reaches a point of no return, we move into the zone of constant irritability and discontent with each other. From there we either go into silent separations, or we reach a point where the possibility of a breakdown in the relationships becomes imminent. Briefly then, as per our current understanding, our relationships go bad because of:

- What we say to each other – the content of our message.
- How we behave and act with each other – the various gestures, the attitude, and the actions that accompany our speech.

The Re-Makings: Our current reconciliation process for remedying the fractured relationship is almost in line with our thinking on how and why our relationships go bad. In the most simplistic terms, the process consists of the following steps:

- Discussing with each other on what was said or done (the message, the behavior, the action) that caused the dissensions.
- Accepting our fault – that what was said or done was not right or appropriate.
- Retracting or withdrawing the unwanted language or behavior.
- Saying sorry – it won't happen again.
- Making up and hoping to be happy ever after.

Typically, this is the process we use to reconcile our fractured relationships. This may involve either a direct one-to-one interplay between the two parties at odds; or it may involve the help, intervention, or mediation of a relative or a friend. In the worst case scenario, it may necessitate the intervention of a counsellor or a psychologist.

The New Perspective

The Breakings: The concept, as per our current understanding, that the modes and mediums of speech and behavior are the agents that break our relationships, is not adequate. They cannot do so, because they are simply inert entities – they are merely tools and instruments that initiate, instigate, and inflate the relationship brawl. They are not, by themselves, the causing agents and, therefore, are not the ones that can be held directly responsible for the ultimate breakdown of the relationship.

Here, then, is my first "new paradigm". The mediums of speech and behavior are, typically, the mouthpiece for somebody else – for some higher faculty inside us – who is the real culprit behind all of this and who is the one responsible for generating and dictating these entities of speech and behavior.

That real culprit is "you" – the "person".

We forget that there is a "person" behind all this melodrama. He is the one who creates and controls all the actions that transpire during relationship confrontations. He is the one who misunderstands or misinterprets the intentions, and has the ego-sensitive personality that plagues the relationship harmony. A relationship is an interaction between two persons – not between two mouths or two actions. When a relationship suffers a setback, it is not the mouth that is to be blamed, it is "you" – the "person" – that is to be held responsible because it is you who is asking the mouth to say something, or commanding the body to behave in a certain way – it is your ego-arrogance that controls your actions. The mediums of speech and behavior are simply the tools of interplay between the two personalities – between the two "persons". Consequently, it is not the entities of speech and behavior that we need to pursue for the sake of bringing permanent relationship harmony, it is the "person" – the "personality" – we have to amend to achieve lasting peace in relationships.

The Re-Makings: The next thing to report is that our current reconciliation processes and practices are weak and inadequate simply because their emphasis is limited only to correcting and amending the entities of relationship interplay. The reconciliation process that we saw above involved making the two conflicting parties sit together and discuss what was said or done that caused dissensions in their relationship and ameliorating the situation through mutual acceptance and agreement. The mediator only goes as far as correcting the entities of behavior – nothing more – nothing less.

There is nothing wrong with the process, it is just that it only provides a temporary reprieve over a limited – confrontation-by-confrontation – span of time and the relationship goes into the same spasm once again at the next confrontation and every subsequent confrontation thereafter.

This is because the entities of speech and behavior are a moving target – they can keep repeating or changing themselves in different shapes and forms over different confrontations. As such, you can come out of one such reconciliation session completely happy and satisfied, but not even a week or so goes by and you are back to your naggings and bickerings again. And, once again, you end up in the reconciliation session, which means that the process needs to be repeated over and over again. And when that happens too often, you reach a point of no return – where the relationship either goes into a spasm of silent separations or goes into the zone of breakings – and you are looking for help all over again.

Here then is my second "new paradigm": you need to amend the "person" and not the entities of behavior, because your relationship is with a live entity – the person – who is influenced by his personality profile. To do that, you have to find out what particular factors impact his profile and his overall behavior and try to systematically amend those factors. Once you have accomplished this task, you would now have a rejuvenated conciliatory person, who would be most conducive and most anxious to seek harmony and happiness in the relationship.

The Person – The Personality

We now come to the final question: "Who is this person we are talking about, and how do we re-invent this person?" This is where the story gets complicated. A person is a very complex being. The person is dictated by his mind, feelings and emotions, and a host of personality characteristics, some inherited by birth, others acquired during interaction with the society we live in. All of these entities collectively impinge upon the person to give him a profile with which he interacts with others.

Recapitulating our new understanding, we can see that the basic entity that affects our relationships is "anger". Anger is generated by the annoyances resulting from our behavioral oddities of speech, attitude and behavior, that we encounter in our day-to-day interactions and confrontations. As the annoyances continue, the anger and antagonism keeps building up slowly and systematically. At times, you don't even know that the other person is accumulating anger inside. The extent of relationship discord and disharmony is directly proportional to the extent of the inside anger we have hoarded. The more the anger, the worst the relationship. When the anger reaches a very high point, the relationship goes into a spasm, leading to a breakdown. What causes behavioral oddities, and hence anger – it's our personality? So then, what we need to find out is which personality characteristics influences our behavior. There are a very large number of personality characteristics that impinge upon our behavior and shape our thinking to give us our specific profile – a persona. To study the characteristics of this phenomenon, I am including, in this book, the following twelve most important personality-behavior factors that I think exert the most profound influence on our person, and hence, on our relationships:

1. Silent Stress
2. Mental-Tape
3. Variety
4. Righteousness
5. Ego
6. Aggressiveness
7. Maturity
8. Thinking
9. Anger
10. Fantasy
11. Expectations
12. Fulfilment

What we need to understand for each of these personality traits is the following:

- How does the characteristic impact our behavior?
- What is our total profile vis-à-vis the collective impact of these factors?
- How do we bring about requisite personality changes?

Re-Inventing the Person

Once we are able to clearly understand what makes us "us" – and what determines and influences the way we behave in relationships – the next step is to "reinvent" our selves, which involves a two-step process: "Awakening" and "Inner-Evolution".

Awakening involves the following three steps:

- Awareness: Knowing what you are and how you behave
- Acceptance: Accepting your shortcomings
- Passion: Desire and determination to enhance your "self"

Inner-evolution involves the following three steps:
- Knowing the self
- Knowing the other
- Passion for harmony

The final goal, indeed, is to create a new "you" – one that would always create positive and happy mediums of speech and behavior – one that would create a milieu of love and togetherness in the relationship – one that would always maintain permanent relationship harmony throughout the life of the relationship.

The New Reconciliation

After having gone through the above process of rejuvenation, you would achieve a state of mind that would take you to a zone of "new reconciliation". In this state, you not only explore the surface – the entities – to ameliorate the relationship harmony, but go deep down into your psyche – your personality – to find out where the anger is and which personality factor is impeding your efforts of achieving harmony. Once you know that, then you can make source-level changes to your profile. This is the new reconciliation process that would, hopefully, be needed only once because its impact will be permanent – final.

Synopsis: The New Paradigms

Logistics Paradigms

For better understanding of the nature of makings and breakings of relationships, the domain must be expanded to include all categories of relationships: marital, silent separations, and the relationship of relatives, because there is a strong inter and intra affect of all relationship-types on each other.

Main Paradigms

1. Although, the behavioral oddities, such as – bad speech and bad attitude, behavior and actions do act as the initiators and instigators that cause relationship annoyances and discord, they are not the entities responsible for the break-up of a relationship. The real causing agent, responsible for the failure of the relationship, is you, the person, and your personality, that generates those behavioral oddities.

2.   The focus of the reconciliation process should, therefore, be not on correcting the entities of behavior only, but on amending the "person-personality" – so that source-level changes can be made to the personality in order to rejuvenate the person for permanent relationship happiness.

2
SILENT SEPARATIONS

"When a glass breaks, everybody hears;
When a heart breaks, nobody hears."

In the previous chapter, I propounded two new "logistics paradigms". In the first one, I introduced a new category that has so far been totally ignored in any discussions of relationship issues – I annotated it as the "silent separations field". The second paradigm emphasized the importance of the category of relatives in the relationship domain, for better understanding of relationship issues. With these additions, I created an expanded relationship field to study our basic problem – why do relationships fail? Since these two entries are rather new, but important, I would like to spend a bit more time on elaborating these new paradigms, before embarking on my journey to elaborate my new perspectives on why relationships go bad, and how we can reconcile them on a permanent basis.

Silent separations

What are silent separations?

What can be a more befitting and appropriate way to express the syndrome of silent separations, than to express it through the feelings of my friend Robert, who once said to me:

> **"I was lonely, so I got married,**
> **Now, we are two lonely people."**

> **"At night when we sleep together in our beds,**
> **It feels as if two graves are lying side by side."**

What a relationship?

Silent separations is a term that I have coined for that category of relationships in which people are still living together in the relationship

– still bounded by the obligations of the relationship, but their love and empathy for each other is almost non-existent. They are physically together, for all intents and purposes, but mentally they are far away from each other. And this is, perhaps, the most prevalent category of the human relationship domain all across the world. Here are some features that depict silent separations:

- There is an eerie calm in your relationship
- A chill
- An uncomfortable silence
- An unseen distance
- An inexplicable loneliness
- An unspoken antagonism and anger
- A life full of silent sobs and dry tears
- An unending nameless pain
- So near, yet so far from each other
- An inexplicable repulsion
- A powerful desire to uphold your own separate and independent identity - where you are you – me is me – you are not "of me" – you are the other - we are together – but only two gathered to remain as two – not as one.

Let us now look at some silent separations scenarios in the context of a marital relationship:

- You feel lonely and lonesome, even when you are together in the same house.
- There is a silent distance between you two.
- It feels like you are sore with each other almost continuously.
- You try to keep yourself busy in your own separate things, rather than things that bring you together.
- You try to avoid direct eye contact with each other.
- He is busy with his work – you are busy with your facials and spas.
- He is working downstairs on his computer – you are reading your book upstairs.
- You do go together to a restaurant every once in a while, but it is as if two mutes are sitting opposite the same table.
- There is almost nothing you agree on, and almost everything you disagree on.

- There is either a constant interplay of naggings and bickerings in your daily life, or there are silent, antagonistic, anger-filled sulkings inside you.
- Your routine interaction is generally filled with contempt, anger, satirical responses, or attempts to put the other down.
- Whenever you are in a social gathering together, you criticize, negate, and pick on each other in front of everyone present. And you attempt to put the other down, intentionally or unintentionally, to prove that you are right – always right.
- Mutual family discussions or discussions relating to family matters, routinely end up in disaster, and the unresolved anger throws you into a relationship spasm. You give each other the "royal silent" treatment – for days, you don't speak with each other, but sulk in silent separations.
- At times, you feel you married the wrong person.
- You feel that others' spouses are nicer, gentler, and more caring – yours is not.
- People can almost read your faces and guesstimate the failing health of your relationship.

Silent separation is not only the disease of the marital-type relationship, it equally affects other types of relationships as well. Here are a few silent separation scenarios in the context of relationships other than marital relationships:

- There are constant, anger-filled feelings and misunderstandings between you and your brothers.
- Your sister-in-law is always sore with you, for no reason that you know of.
- How is it that your mother-in-law is always right?
- Your wife thinks you listen too much to your mother – your mother thinks you listen too much to your wife – and you are hopelessly and helplessly sandwiched between the two.
- There is an unspoken distance between you and your friends.

This is just a random sample of some familiar mini scenarios of silent separations. They are not for you, you, and you – they are for all of us – we are all into this rut together – we are all party to the process.

These scenarios are indicative of unhappy, unhealthy, failing relationships that set the tone for silent separations or for the ultimate failure of relationships.

My observations and research, over a long span of time, have provided me with enough testimony to be able to say, with utmost certainty, that the magnitude of this problem is very close to epidemic proportions. Every place that I looked around, I found people quietly suffering from this nameless pain of unhappy togetherness. And I am sure that you must also have encountered similar scenarios in your own circle of friends and relatives.

The problem is, indeed, more pronounced and noticeable in the arena of marital relationships, where I found many a husband and wife still living "together", but as two strangers. They seem to be stuck in the relationship – not daring to break the relationship, and not wanting to live into the relationship either – though still busy nagging and criticizing each other on anything and everything. And I asked myself: "Are these the same two people who courted and loved each other so passionately at the time of the consummation their marriage"? So what went wrong?

It is absolutely astounding to see that, despite the magnanimity of the problem, no one has ever recognized and identified this issue of silent separations as a separate and special entity. There is no book that makes even a passing mention of this lot. There is no scholar or professional who has ever raised or debated this critical aspect of relationships. I personally think that it is an issue of grave significance and it deserves our full attention. We don't mean to consider this category just because it has not received any attention before, but we know that its consideration will add much more information that would help us to understand our basic issue more clearly – "why relationships fail".

To prove my point, I would pose a simple question: "Why do one group of people – the silent separations type, for example – still hang on to each other, and not break, while the other, the marital type, ends up breaking the relationship, when in both scenarios the couple goes through the same regimen of bad speech and bad behavior?" What is that one underlying factor that influences the situation? The answer will bring you back to my new paradigm – that it is the "person" – the "personality" – that plays the biggest part in the breakdown of relationships. In one case, the couple overrides and controls, to some extent, their personality characteristics that influence their decisions, while in the other case, they let their personality factors control their actions of separation. This, indeed, reinforces the prowess of my new findings: that in order to bring a state of permanent harmony and happiness, you need to control and enhance those of your personality factors that impinge upon the interplay of your relationships.

Relative-Type Relationships

Let me now elaborate on the role and importance of the second and equally-significant facet – the relationship of relatives. To a large extent, we have so far ignored the consideration of this category in the greater relationship domain, at least to the extent of its comparison with marital-type relationships.

To start with, let us look at the various types of relationships that we encounter in our life. They are: marital or marital-type, relatives, friends, business, other socio-business relationships.

Of these, the first one, the "marital-type", is perhaps the most important of all. I personally consider this as the nucleus of all relationships – the one from which all other relationships emanate or merge into. This type will be the main focus of our discussion in this book. Basically, the marital-type category includes: relationship of husband and wife, as well as all other types of such and similar relationships, formal or informal, consummated or non-consummated.

Problems and breakdowns in this type of relationships are a consequence of the following forces:
- Internal Behavior Aspects
  - How we connect with each other
  - How positively or negatively we interact
  - The compatibility of our personality, thinking, and behavior patterns
  - The making or not-making of our mental perceptions and the accumulation of feelings of anger.
- External Circumstances and Interventions
  - Matters of conflict arising out of discord between or because of children
  - Conflicts arising out of interventions of relatives and possibly of friends.

Of course, as you know, I have enhanced and expanded the scope of this relationship to include both categories of problems: the actual physical breakdowns, as well as the silent separations breakdowns.

Now, coming back to the category of relative-type relationships, we can see that it includes all those relationships that come into being either by virtue of our birth or by virtue of marriage. While marital relationships can be broken due to any number of problems – internal to the relationship or external vis-à-vis other relationships – the relationship with relatives cannot be broken. The most you can do is put the relationship into a temporary or permanent limbo. For example, if you are son of William, you may spoil your relationship with your father or even try to break it, yet everyone would still address you as the "son of William" – or son of William, who doesn't speak to his father anymore. Even when your father dies, people would still say: he is the son of William who died last year.

Problems with and within the confines of relatives, normally, occur due to one or more of the following reasons:

- Interference in the primary relationship
- Unreasonable levels of expectations
- Personality differences
- Differences in thinking, behavior, and actions

Over and above the fact that this category is important in its own right, as it encompasses the bulk of our lifelong relationships, its importance is especially of greater significance because of the following:

- A large majority of the time the core marital relationship suffers its demise, whether in silent separations or through actual physical breakings, due to the direct or indirect intervention, interference and alienation with relatives. It is, therefore, obvious that we must understand the anatomy of the breakings of the relationship of relatives in order to understand more clearly the nature of the breakings of the core marital relationship.

- The inclusion of the category of relatives will also authenticate and enhance our new paradigm of "person-personality". Our current theory asserts that the interplay of the entities of behavior in our confrontations causes problems. But then, what about the situation where you nephew hates you even when he has never interacted with you. And he hates you because his father hates you. It means that the nephew is mentally interacting with you on the basis of perception that he has formed about you. This authenticates our new paradigm, that it is the person-personality that plays the dominant role in relationship interactions. As a matter of fact, most of us interact with each other on the basis of our own built-up impressions and perceptions about the other. This is the mental-tape effect that I shall further elaborate on in the proceeding chapter.

So as you can see, our present framework, by itself, is really not sufficient enough to adequately explain why our relationships go bad. And a comparative analysis and understanding of why all relationship-types fail – especially those of the relatives and of the silent separations category – would provide us with better and more reliable answers to the dilemma. This really brings me back to reinforcing my new assertion: that it is not only our behavior, but also our whole personality, that determines how our relationships would function and harmonize.

With this brief introduction, I am now ready to go into my main premise – my new paradigm about relationships – and the proceeding chapters are dedicated to elucidate the entire conceptual framework of my new thoughts.

SECTION 2
GROUND ZERO
THE UNDERSTANDING

3
RELATIONSHIPS: A REALITY CHECK

"It takes a whole life-time to make a relationship;
It takes just the blink of the eye to break it."

With this chapter, we now begin our discussion of the subject in a more systematic manner. This chapter is simply devoted to dialoguing the role and necessity of relationships to life – which is the first and most important step towards understanding the nature of relationships.

Life Equals Relationships

Human life!!! We don't know where we came from – we don't know where we go when life ends – we don't even know the true purpose of life. Among the many "don't knows", what we do know is that we get only one trip through life and that trip is intricately interwoven with all types of relationships, or, more succinctly, life is simply a sum total of relationships. In fact, life equals relationships. Relationships are the lifeline of our life.

What is a relationship? A relationship is merely an interactive interplay between two or more persons. Relationships are the means and mediums of life through which we connect and interact with each other to lead life. As such, therefore, life and relationships are irrevocably intertwined – they are inseparable – one cannot exist without the other. Take away relationships from life and life may either not survive in some situations, or it may be almost meaningless or empty.

Despite That

If that is so, then I guess it would be natural to expect that living in harmonious relationships would be an absolute necessity. True, but unfortunately this is not the case – you know it and I know it. Pity – despite this overwhelming importance and compulsive necessity of relationships to life, it is virtually incomprehensible to see how easily we break our relationships, either physically (broken relationships) or mentally (silent separations). In the flicker of a mere thought, we are ready to destroy forever, or put into permanent limbo, a relationship that we spend almost a lifetime building. And generally for what – a simple spoken word – an unintentional gesture – or a meaninglessly trivial behavioral mistake.

Look around you and you would see that people are breaking their relationships left, right, and center – and without any remorse or feelings of guilt. And, these breakdowns are neither restricted to the periods of our life span, nor limited to the type of relationships. Marital relationships are breaking-up at every stage of marital life – early after marriage – midway through – or even in old age. And this is happening with complete disregard of the fact that children may be involved in the process and may get hurt because of this dilemma. It takes us more time to find a suitable partner than it takes to break the relationship. Even in the relative-type relationships – where breakings are neither possible nor an option – people are sore with each other, thus keeping their relationships in limbo, whether temporary or permanent.

Have you ever noticed how quickly and easily we get angry with each other over matters that are, at times, so ridiculously trivial and unimportant? It is as if we are always sitting on the virtual edge of emotionality – where with one little tilt, our ego falls off the emotional cliff – bingo! The result: relationship bankruptcy. It's almost a laughing matter. I am sure you can recount hundreds of scenarios of your own where your disagreements with your spouse or relatives were truly the result of meaninglessly trivial annoyances, and yet it jolted your relationship. The problem is not the triviality of each of those actions in isolation – the problem is that these angry individual confrontations lead to the formation of a cumulative effect – the mental-tape of misunderstandings and antagonistic feelings – that ultimately becomes instrumental in destroying the relationship harmony.

I asked myself the question: "Is fighting a given with us?" Is it a sort of thing that is built-in in our genetic make-up? It seems so. To fight, we don't have to work very hard – it's always there around the corner. But, to make-up, or to generate a good relationship, we really have to work hard. In any case, the thing to think about is: "Is this what life is all about? Is this the purpose of life, to fight, to bicker, to nag each other over stupid little things – worthless entities – especially when we have only one life to live, and we know that relationships are a required part of that life?" Must that bickering only end with death, can't it end within the living span of life? Funny – during the living span of our life, we fight with each other, but when the other person dies, we cry over the loss. Why can't we give each other the same love and compassion during our live-togetherness that we give each other when we are separated by death or otherwise?

The Irony: Relationship 101

It is totally baffling to see that, despite this unequivocal need for relationships in our life and living, nowhere during our upbringing or in our entire life for that matter, are we ever taught, formally or informally, the anatomy and physiology of relationships. This is a subject that each one of us learns in our own way, simply as a by-product of growing up. And we surely do a pretty lousy job.

The irony is that we learn everything else, formally, in our lives – science, arts, engineering, medicine, languages, music, etc. – but not the subject that we know is the most important of all for our life and living – "maintaining relationships". Shouldn't this subject be at the top of every curriculum – at every stage of our learning process – "Compulsory: Relationships 101".

No Wonder

No wonder, therefore, when things go wrong in our relationships, we are totally incapable of resolving our simplest human misunderstandings. Being ill-prepared for the task, our first pursuit begins with looking for external help to resolve our internal dilemma. Depending on the nature and seriousness of the relationship discord, the external help and intervention may come from a relative, a friend, or in the worst-case scenario, we may seek the help or mediation of a counsellor or a psychologist.

What a strange and paradoxical dichotomy – that, on one hand, we (our ego) thinks that we know all – and we are always right – and on the other hand, we beg for external help. We become totally helpless when it comes to resolving a simple emotional issue, and that too, relating to people we love or are supposed to love.

There is, of course, nothing wrong with seeking external help. As a matter of fact, it is vitally helpful in a situation where you are, yourself, the directly-emotionally-involved party. When you, yourself, are involved, you are emotionally charged-up – you can't see things in their right perspective – your mental lens is temporarily fogged-up with your own emotions and feelings. In such a situation, mentors do have a role to play – and a very important one. But, what you need to understand is the following:

- That, mentors don't have a magic wand to whip through a solution for a highly emotional issue such as this – one that is totally personal to you. They are also human beings like you and they do not understand human emotions any more or any less than you do. Or at least they cannot understand your internal, personal feelings and emotions any more or better than you can.

- That, you cannot just step aside and say – ah ha! The mentors are here – they will solve the whole dilemma for me – I don't have to do anything. Sorry to disappoint you – it's your game – you are the involved party – you have to be fully involved and a willing participant in any counselling process – you have to be the active player in the process.

- That, external help and intervention does and can play a useful role in reconciling the fractured relationship, yet the external help can only act as a catalyst in awakening your own internal wisdom and resolve – which may, perhaps, have been temporarily dormant inside you. So, it is evident that you do have to have your own inner wisdom and resolve in the first place. If you have it, the outside help would be effective. If you don't have it – or if it is permanently dormant – or if you don't make your own efforts to awaken it – then no amount of external help can do you any good. And a further point to note is that, ultimately, if the external help proves to be useful, you have to know that it was not just the magic of external help only – it was because you always had what it takes to reconcile inside you, and that external help simply acted as a catalyst.

Let me close the discussion with a simple thought. A relationship is simply a matter of two persons, you and the other. Its health depends on: how you connect with each other, how you treat each other, how you understand each other's feelings, how sensitive you are to each other's needs, and so on. The harmony of your relationship is measured by the distance between you two, that is, the "mental distance". The greater the distance, the unhappier your relationship, even when it is physically intact. So, what you need to understand is: why and how this distance is created, and how to eliminate it.

This distance is created by your mental thoughts, feelings, and perceptions about the "other". As long as you keep thinking that "the other is other", you would maintain that the "other" is different – and this would bring a feeling in you that the "other" is unacceptable or bad. Not until you start thinking that the "other" is not "other" but is like you – your own – will you begin to reduce that distance. So, the first thing you have to do is to "stop thinking that the other is other".

When is the "other" other? Only when you don't know the "self". The moment you know the "self", you find that the "other" is the same as the "self" – that there are no two entities: "self and the other"– they are both one and the same – and the distance disappears.

Therefore, the key is to know the "self". When you find your "self" – and find out that it is not bad or hell – then you will find that the other is also as beautiful, and is not hell – because your "self" and the "other" are now one and the same thing. This argument defies the logic of **Jean Paul Sartre**, the French philosopher. One of his famous sayings is that: **"Hell is the other person"**, also commonly known as: **"The other is hell"**. My personal rebuttal to that is as follows:

"The other is not hell;

It is your own thinking that the other is hell, that is hell."

This is what I call "humble surrenders" – the path to relationship harmony.

4

THE MAKINGS AND BREAKINGS OF RELATIONSHIPS

"Relationships break because of what you do;
But, what you do is because of what you are."

In Chapter 1, I presented a new vision – a new and uniquely different perspective on relationships. Being an introductory chapter, the discussion was limited to a panoramic overview of the subject. I shall now continue where I left off and provide a more detailed and systematic account of the new vision in this chapter.

Relationships are an issue of immense significance to our life and living. This is what was amply emphasized in the preceding chapters. If human life is the most important entity on this planet, then human relationships are the next most significant facet of life. Relationships are an inherent necessity of life – one cannot exist without the other. If that is so, then I guess it would be natural to expect that living in harmonious relationships should be an absolute necessity for us all. True, but unfortunately that is not the case – you know it and I know it. Absolutely astounding, isn't it? We know we have to live into relationships – and we, of course, do – but we spend our whole life fighting with each other – and that too, generally, for simple emotional issues.

Why is it so – why does it seem that we are continuously sore with each other? Why this unseen distant between us – a feeling of ego-arrogance to protect our individuality and self-esteem – wanting to be together, yet endeavouring to uphold our "me-ness" – why this perplexing dichotomy? These are some of the pressing questions about relationships that have continuously defied us, and we still don't have the answers. It's a complex dilemma, of course, because it involves a complex entity – the human person. Notwithstanding however, I am attempting to put forth a new vision that our current thinking has not been able to provide, which I hope will provide you with some viable alternatives and solutions to the dilemma.

The Main Goals

The two major questions that confront us with regard to the issue of failing relationships are:

1. Breakings: Why do our relationships fail?
2. Re-Makings: Why are our reconciliation processes incapable of bringing in a permanent sense of harmony in our relationship breakdowns? Why are we wrapped up in the unending cycle of "makings – breakings – re-makings – re-breakings ..." of relationships?

In the same breath, the next intelligent question, therefore, is: "Why have we been unable to resolve the dilemma of failing relationships thus far – especially when we have researched the subject so immensely, and we have so much knowledge and professional help at hand?" Are we missing some key indicators, or do we have some gaps and deficiencies in our current understanding and practices?

I am sure many of you who also have as much genuine interest and inquisitiveness in the subject as I have must also be asking the same questions. You must also be making concerted efforts to understand the nature of relationships. You must have gone over the entire literature – you must have discussed the issue of relationships with many close friends, relatives, or even with some counsellors and/or psychologists. Or, to put it more succinctly, you have done everything that you possibly could do and yet, you still feel that there is a void inside you – a gap in your understanding on why relationships fail. As a matter of fact, you have that uncanny feeling inside you that the harder you work on your relationships, the more behind you get. You find yourself stagnant on a moving rail as if life is passing by and you are not able to grab hold of it, despite your best efforts and intentions. Sound familiar? Don't worry – you are not alone.

This lack of precise answers to the dilemma, and the obvious helplessness of our current systems to adequately resolve the issue, served as a powerful incentive for my research. After considerable contemplation, focused research and observations, I was able to achieve a breakthrough into the problem. A new perspective, ultimately, manifested itself – a new vision was born. From my findings, I came to the simple, but painful, conclusion that the fundamental reason why we are unable to resolve the dilemma of failing relationships, is because our present understanding of why relationships fail, and our current reconciliation processes, are seriously deficient and inadequate. Although it was a difficult task to challenge the entire framework of our well-established current system, it was not too difficult to reach this conclusion – for, as I said to myself, and I may even ask you:

- That if our current understanding is complete and correct, then why are we still grappling with the issue?
- That if our current process of reconciliation is sound, then why are we still unable to break out of the unending cycle of "makings and breakings" of relationships, to establish permanent relationship harmony despite our best efforts and intentions and despite the bountiful knowledge and literature we have.

Although, the initial intent and focus of my research was only to find viable answers to the two main questions appended above, the whole process automatically highlighted some secondary paradigms identifying various other key deficiencies and weaknesses of the current system. Basically, the following four fundamental shortcomings were brought to light from which some unique alternative options and solutions manifested themselves.

The Shortcomings

1. Magnitude: That our estimate of the extent and magnitude of the problem is incomplete.
2. Dimension: That our current focus on the dimensions of different types of relationships is very narrow and inadequate.
3. Breakings: That our present understanding of how and why relationships go bad, is a bit off-track and deficient.
4. Re-Makings: That our present approach to reconciliation is quite weak and inadequate.

The first two findings relate to the logistics of the relationship domain and the last two to the core issue – that of makings and breakings of relationships. We shall examine these deficiencies one by one.

The New Paradigms of Magnitude and Dimension

Starting with the first one – the paradigm of "magnitude" pertains to the extent of the problem. We all know that there is a crisis in our relationships – but what we don't know is how big the crisis is.

Don't believe them when they tell you that the rate of separations and/or divorces, in most industrialized western countries is almost close to fifty percent (50%) – it's not true – it's really close to ninety percent (90%) – and rising.

If you think that's ridiculous, think again. It's neither ridiculous nor funny – it is a silent reality – an unspoken truth.

Well then! Who are those additional forty percent (40%) that I am adding on? They are those unfortunate broken hearts that are still buried, most unhappily, but quietly, under the gloom and doom of unbroken relationships. They are the ones who are still living together – or living side-by-side, rather than together – bounded by the shackles of relationship obligations. They are hopelessly and lovelessly hanging loose in limbo relationships. They are suffering from what I annotate as the "silent separations" – the broken hearts in unbroken relationships" – the "lonesome togetherness", which is even worse than the real thing – the actual "breakings". They are the ones who are unable to break the relationship – for one reason or another – and they also do not want to stay in the relationship either.

The birthing of a new conceptual framework – this was my first new revelation.

And by the way, this trend is not exclusive to only the westernized countries; it is equally spread across all continents. In many countries, the problem of silent separations, for example, is even more pronounced because: one, they are going through the growing pains of becoming westernized; two, their tight infrastructure of customs does not allow the freedom of seeking separations and divorces.

Our current literature had completely missed this issue, perhaps because we have been overly preoccupied with only one aspect of failing relationships – that of actual physical separation and divorce, and that too only in the context of one type of relationship, the marital type. Why did this happen? Perhaps because of the fact that the facet of divorces is open and visible, and all kinds of information is readily available. On the other hand, the facet of silent separations is less pronouncedly manifested, and is more obscure, unseen, subtle, and hidden, because there are no statistics available on it.

Incidentally, if we closely examine the silent separation category, we can, of course, see that this category is not really a separate entity; it is an integral part of the same relationship – the marital group. They are just two faces of the same coin – one that openly manifests its problems and moves towards actual physical separations and divorces, and the other that doesn't openly manifest its disharmony, but instead silently suffers in the relationship without breaking it. Whether invisible and subtle, or part of the same group, when I looked around I found that a very large majority of relationships are, sort of, secretly suffering and suffocating in unspoken silent separations. I found innumerable number of couples living together in relationships, even when they are unhappy in the relationship. They cannot break the relationship, for one reason or another, and at the same time, they don't want to stay in the relationship either.

Surprisingly, nobody talks about these people, nobody is even vaguely aware of this lot. Is it that sensitive an issue, is it our own idiosyncrasy. Is it an honest and unintentional slip of the mind, or is it lack of awareness? There is no book that makes a mention of this category of people, as well there is no human-behavior scholar who has ever identified or raised this issue, howsoever vaguely or remotely. And this is despite the fact that the syndrome of silent separations is far more prevalent, as well as more painful, than the syndrome of real breakings.

Even putting it in the context of the 50-40 split that I mentioned above, when you think of it, silent separations are not the sufferings of only the additional forty percent (40%) – it is really the anguish of the entire ninety percent (90%) – or perhaps of the whole population. How is that so? Well! The fifty percent that would go through the actual physical separation or divorce, would perhaps, start establishing new relationships once again. Given the onslaught of time, they may consequently end up breaking the relationship again and get trapped in the same morbid chasm of "silent separations" all over again.

And speaking of silent separations as being more painful than real breakings, you can easily see that in the case of real breakings, given the benefit of time, you get over the pain, and then you start rebuilding new relationships all over again. But with silent separations, you are stuck in an unhappy relationship – you can't break through, for one reason or another – you are trapped. And consequently, you are constantly hurting – it's an unending streak of anguish, anger, frustration, sulkings, depression, and so on.

Actually, silent separations, in themselves, are a powerful indicator of an impending relationship disaster. They are a birthing platform for all relationship problems. So not only are silent separations themselves painful, they are also the steps that may ultimately lead to actual physical separations. As a matter of fact, the facet of separations and divorces is really a by-product of silent separations. All separations are preceded by silent separations and all divorces or remakings may again end up in silent separations.

The inclusion of this new category will provide us with much more information that would help us to better understand why relationships fail. We can verify this fact by asking a very simple question: why do relationships completely break in one case, while they stay in limbo in the other, when in both situations the persons and the confrontational situations are identical. And the answer will be that it is a decision of the person and his personality, and not of the entities of speech and behavior.

Let me now touch upon the other paradigm – the paradigm of "dimension" – that is concerned with the relationship of "relatives". Like the "silent separations" category, we have also equally left out and ignored this important facet of our relationships, and once again you can see that very little has been written or debated about this aspect of relationships as well. The inclusion of the relationship of relatives is important because a large majority of marital relationships suffer from silent separations or breakdowns mainly due to the interventions and alienation arising from the relationship of relatives.

The inclusion of this category in the mainframe of the relationship domain would, indeed, enhance our understanding of why relationships fail. When we speak of breakings, it is, of course, associated with marital relationships, because the relationship of relatives cannot break – the most you can do is to put it in limbo. But I personally believe that putting a relationship in permanent limbo or breaking it are both equally painful – they are all breakings. In that context, if we ask the question again: why do relationships with relatives break, we would once again realize that it is because of the person's personality – which once again validates my new paradigm.

These two facets of magnitude and dimension that I have elucidated above would now help us establish a new and expanded relationship field – one that encompasses all categories of relationships. From here onwards, therefore, this expanded field is the one that we shall be dealing with in the remainder of the book.

The Paradigms of Breakings and Reconciliations

Let us now examine the other two items – the core issues – of "breakings and re-makings" of relationships. We shall first examine our current perspective on the issues, identify the inadequacies of the current approach, and then outline our new vision.

The Current Understanding

The Breakings: Why do our relationships go bad and break? Our relationships, indeed, go bad because of many things, but on a confrontation-by-confrontation basis, they go sour because of how we behave and act with each other during our relationship interplay. That is, what we say to each other (the speech – the content of our message), and how we behave (the various gestures, attitudes, and actions that accompany our speech). In our routine conversations, we say things to each other or extend an attitude that reflects our intentions. And if the nature of those intentions is not acceptable to the other, or is not to his/her liking or expectations, a wave of displeasure and anger runs through the other person's mind. Congratulations! A dissension has taken birth. Now, if you repeat this type of scenario, over and over again, in successive confrontations over time, you can well imagine what will happen – a cumulative, anger-filled, antagonistic mindset would be generated. And a continuous state of such a mindset would have a high probability of creating disharmony, or even breakdown.

Let me now go over a routine scenario of the process of breakings – and to make the discussion more realistic, I will consider the example of you and your spouse. We shall start with the very first confrontational incidence and build the scenario from there:

- There is an argument, or a discussion in the house – between you two – on a certain issue. It may be something relating to attitude, behavior, an action that any one of you has taken, an issue involving children, or an issue relating to an intervention by any of your common relatives.
- You exchange information, views, feelings and emotions with each other.

- Nothing is resolved, and your conversation ends in limbo.
- A feeling of anger, irritability, and frustration has taken birth.
- Over and above, you may have, inadvertently, said something to your spouse that, presumably, was not very nice.
- According to your understanding and recollection, you don't remember to have said anything derogatory.
- Not according to your spouse, unfortunately – she may have interpreted your remarks as rude or sarcastic.
- Her feelings are hurt – and she is angry with you.
- She may show her anger or she may hide it inside. If she shows her anger and discontent – it should be very good – because at least you would come to know that she is angry and you would try to communicate and generate a dialogue to resolve the misunderstanding. If, on the other hand, she hides it, it may, unfortunately, lead to a build-up effect and create damage at a later date.
- In any case, a bad feeling has taken birth – the first seed of discontentment has been sown – the relationship has taken a direct hit.
- At this point in time, perhaps, you don't even know if she is angry or hurt or felt bad about what you said. You didn't even attempt to find out if she is annoyed because, according to you, what you said was really trivial, meaningless, and without any bad feelings or intentions. And you are not even aware that she is angry or that the relationship has taken a hit. You go along with your life as if nothing has happened.
- Indeed there are subtle indicators, if you can look for them, which can tell you that your spouse is angry with you. For example, there can be an uncalled for silence in your interactions, more than it normally should be, or, there can be an unusual increase in your routine bickerings and naggings.
- Of course, the damage, if any, can be controlled right here and now if both of you can realize the presence of an unspoken anger, and you both try to communicate and clarify the misunderstanding – say sorry – and make up with each other.
- If not, then there is a strong possibility that the incidence would be recorded on your spouse's mental-tape (a concept to

be discussed later), and a bad set of feelings would be archived permanently.

- This is the story of a single confrontational incidence. Although, a single incidence may seem to be of little significance, but it can certainly become the first sign of an impending disaster.
- The result – an image – an impression – a profile has taken birth – a silent revolution has begun – the wheels of silent antagonism have been set into motion.
- And now imagine and multiply the results of this one single incidence by hundreds and thousands of such confrontational incidences happening over time.
- And imagine something even more dramatic – that you don't even know that a mental-tape is being filled up – slowly – systematically – and that, layer upon layer of antagonistic feelings are being accumulated on the tape.
- Until one fine morning, the sleeping volcano wakes up – the relationship goes into a spasm of either silent separations or actual breakings.

This is just a brief story of how relationships can suffer a setback – this is how a relationship can reach a point of no return – mentally, if not physically. And, many a times, you are not even aware of why it happened – you are simply puzzled – you are saying – what happened – where did we go wrong. Normally, it happens because we fail to recognize what is trivial and what is emotionally damaging until it is too late and the damage has been done.

Briefly then - according to our current understanding, our relationships go bad because of our bad behavioral interactions – that is, because of the bad entities of speech, behavior, and actions. Relationships suffer their setback because of how we display our attitude – our gestures – our persona – our personality profile.

The Reconciliations: Our current reconciliation involves a get-together of the conflicting parties to thrash away the misunderstandings. It may involve one-on-one discussion, or the assistance or mediation of a relative or friend, or, in the worst scenario, it may necessitate the intervention of a counsellor or a psychologist. Irrespective of its format, the process generally goes through this sequence: we sit together face to face with each other and, with the mentor's help, discuss what each one of us said or did that caused dissensions and anger. We accept our fault, retract our stance, say sorry, make a promise that it won't happen again, make up with each other, and live happily ever after.

Not so, unfortunately! Not even a week goes by and we are again at odds with each other. We are back to the bargaining table again and we go through the same reconciliation process again. And like this, the task of reconciliation remains endless: we fight – we reconcile – we fight – we re-reconcile, and so on. The reason for this unending effort is clearly obvious: that the focus of this reconciliation approach is only on correcting the entities of behavior – that is, what we said or did. But unfortunately, entities are fluid in nature – they are a moving target – they constantly change from confrontation to confrontation. It is one thing that you will say on one occasion that creates a dissension, and it may be another behavioral pattern you might display on another occasion that causes dissensions. Thus, a reconciliation process that aims at correcting only the entities, is bound to be infinitely repetitive, and without any positive end-results.

The New Perspective

The Breakings: The first serious weakness of our current thinking emanates from the fact that we uphold the understanding that the entities of speech and behavior, by themselves, are the end-all – the only source of relationship discord. Our new thinking refutes this by arguing that, while the entities of behavior are important and should be closely monitored and amended – they cannot be the ones responsible for the breakdown of the relationship because they are simply inert in nature – they are only the tools and instruments that initiate and instigate the relationship brawl. The entities are simply a mouthpiece for some higher faculty inside us, which is the real culprit behind all this – the one who generates, controls, and dictates our actions of speech and behavior.

That real culprit is "you" – the "person". This is my main new paradigm.

A relationship is an interaction between two persons – two live bodies – not between two mannequins or two attitudes or two mouths. When a relationship suffers a setback, it is not the mouth or the attitude that is to be blamed – it is "you" – the "person" – that is to be held responsible because it is you who is asking the mouth to say something, or commanding the body to display a certain attitude. Attitude, for example, is not independently live and active body – it's an inert entity – and the entities become alive only when you step into it. So it is you who is answerable to all that transpires in the relationship interaction.

What we seem to forget is that, there is a "person" behind all this melodrama. That a relationship is a matter of interplay between two persons, and the way they react, interact, and behave with each other determines how the relationship would materialize and harmonize. The carriers of interplay are, surely, the mediums and modes of speech and behavior. The situation can be compared to a chariot – the body of the chariot being the modes and mediums of interplay, and the driver being the "person". The chariot and its body cannot move without the driver – because the body is an inert entity just like the mediums of behavior. The only consciously live entity that controls the chariot – the relationships – is the driver – the "person". Relationships do not break because of the body of the chariot; they break because of the driver – the person. Consequently, we have to focus our attention to a higher plain of thinking – the plain of the "total person" – and attempt to make amendments in the person to achieve permanent relationship harmony.

While the revelation of this paradigm of the "person", as the key ingredient in the dilemma of relationship breakdowns, was the biggest breakthrough in my findings, there were several other important secondary findings that emerged out of this as a by-product. Some of those are appended below while others will be expounded as we move along in the book.

- Relationships do not go bad only because of what you say. They also go bad, in most of the cases in fact, because of the interpretation the other person draws from what you said. Misinterpretations and misunderstandings are the single most prevalent sources of annoyances of routine relationship interactions. The interpretations by the other person of the intent of what you said hold the key to relationship problems. Most often, those interpretations are a by-product of the person's own thinking and personality.

- Relationships can go bad even without the happening of any confrontational interaction, or without your having said anything bad, or any misinterpretations either. This is so because your mind can generate hypothetical situations through mental imagery, and can create bad relationship situations with another person that you haven't even met or interacted with, and create a war that was not there anyway.

• Relationships can even go bad even when you remain silent, because silence is also construed by the other as an attitude of arrogance. And this can hurt the other person's ego-pride, resulting in the birthing of bad feelings.

The Reconciliations: Looking at the current reconciliation approach, we can now visualize the obvious, but serious, shortcomings in our process. Firstly, the process is faulty simply because of our faulty understanding of why relationships go bad. We consider the modes of speech and behavior, in themselves, as the end, rather than the means to the end. We take these inert entities as the only agents that cause relationship discord – and that makes the reconciliation process inadequate and weak. Indeed, there is nothing wrong with the logistics of the process per se – rather, on the contrary, it is the right thing to do. But, unfortunately, this approach has a very limited impact – it lacks the requisite potency for permanent relationship harmony because its emphasis is only on correcting the symptoms (the entities of speech and behavior) and not the disease (the person himself/herself). This approach does provide us with a temporary reprieve in the breakdown of relationships, but it leaves room for relapse – for the relationship to go back into the same antagonistic abyss once again, upon another confrontation or misunderstanding.

This approach leaves us without answers – or perhaps, with more questions than answers. What do we do the next time we have a relationship upheaval – do we repeat the process? Then how often do we have to repeat and keep repeating this process and stay wrapped-up in the unending cycle of makings and breakings. The solution, of course, is very simple – we have to focus our attention on correcting and amending the source of the problem – the person. Once the "person" is re-invented and rejuvenated, he would not generate unacceptable entities of behavior in the first place, and there would be no cause for relationship disharmony – and reconciliation may either be not needed, or may be required just once.

Incidentally, besides being weak and temporary in nature, our current reconciliation process also has two other serious drawbacks that have not been identified by any writer or practitioner before. First, because the process is transient and only focuses on correcting the entities of behavior, the two parties may, in the desire to get out of this process, give the false impression that they have amicably resolved their outstanding differences when, in fact, they haven't., and down deep inside they are still holding their anger and grudge for each other. Second, this process has the distinct possibility of generating a feeling of hurt-ego – a feeling of let-down – a feeling of defeat and humiliation – which is what both parties may, inadvertently, construe or feel about the reconciliation because the main emphasis of the process is to give in and surrender in order to reconcile. And, if that happens – and I am not saying that it always happens – it can further aggravate the already sensitive inner feelings of the built-up anger. The relationship can then go even deeper into the spasm of silent separations. And, with the transient and temporary nature of our current process, this may happen at each confrontation – and the total build-up of these feelings of hurt-ego over many confrontations may cause irreversible damage to the relationship that may certainly lead to breakings.

The new reconciliation paradigm, therefore, starts the reconciliation process at the person level. And, since a person is a by-product of many personality factors, the process goes down to the person's psyche to explore why relationship dissensions occur in the first place, or why they repetitively occur – and which particular aspects of your personality causes these dissensions. Let me re-state the process:

- The starting point of the process is the same as used in our current approach to reconciliation – a discussion of what was said that caused dissentions and an amicable resolution through mutual clarification, if possible.
- With the old system, the process stopped there – but not with my new paradigm. Here, the process would go further into a deeper level of understanding – a level where you or the mentor – would grope into your and the other person's inner feelings – the inner personality – to find out why the dissensions really happened in the first place, why they happen so frequently, and to locate where the discontentment and anger is hiding – to identify the patters of discordant behavior.

This refurbished approach will bring to light the real causes of your relationship discord and disharmony and if you can resolve these amicably, you will achieve that sense of permanent relationship harmony. This process will be further elaborated in section 5.

Mediums and Modes of Connecting

Earlier, I concluded that the mediums of connecting are simply inert in nature, yet, of course, I also emphasized that they should be properly monitored, and corrected. Now I want to look into this particular aspect in greater detail. To begin with, let's examine the aspects of our being that are directly and constantly involved in the interplay of relationships – they are: the mind, the body, and the emotions. The various mediums and modes through which these three entities function, by virtue of which our relationships go bad, are as follows:

1. Mediums of connecting:
   a. The mouth – the speech: what we say to each other – the content of our message.
   b. The body – the behavior: the behavioral patterns, bodily gestures, and mannerisms that accompany the conveyance of the message.
2. Modes of Behavior: The tone and attitude of our speech and behavior: (a) Positive, (b) Negative, (c) Neutral.
3. The Action: Any physical action that we may take that would be detrimental to the emotional well being of our relationships.

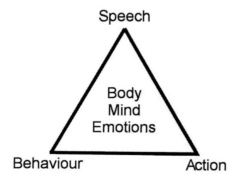

Figure 1 - Mediums and Modes of Connecting

Mind – Body – Emotions

Let me now explain how these entities function. Note that it is not a "Biology 101" course and the explanation that I am putting forth for the role of these entities is by no means a scientific elaboration – or even close to it. I am only presenting it as an amusing anecdote, just to generate an informal dialogue to show how these entities influence our thinking and our behavior patterns. It would be nice to know how these entities function – individually as well as collectively – and how we can coordinate and control their functioning to our relationship advantage. One thing we must keep in mind is that our actions are not the result of any particular singular activity – they are, usually, the result of the collective impact of many entities put together – our speech, our behavior, our thinking, our emotions, our personality, etc. In the same breath, we should remember that relationships, generally, do not go bad because of one single incidence or confrontation of annoyance – unless the nature and intensity of that incidence is highly emotionally-damaging – that relationships go bad because of a collective impact of a multitude of discordant confrontations. With this in mind, let's begin our discussion on the role and interplay of mind, body, and emotions.

Let's begin our discussion of the two interrelationships: mind and body, and mind and emotions. Pairing, first, the mind and body – the question to ask is: does mind control the functioning of, for example, the mouth, eyes, ears, etc. – or are they independent of the mind's control? Take the case of the eyes, for example. Does the mind tell the eyes to see and report back, or do the eyes see things on their own and then report back to the mind (or brain)? What if I close my eyes and do not see anything – what can my mind do – can it force the eyes to open and see. It seems as if the eyes are independent of the mind's control – I know that's not possible because our knowledge tells us that mind is the supreme-most entity that controls everything. Does the mind tell the mouth to speak – or does the mouth pre-empt the mind? The way we speak with each other, at least vis-à-vis our relationship interactions, makes it seem as if the mouth pre-empts the mind. We open our mouths and utter things way faster than the mind's capability to tell the mouth what to say. Put it more bluntly – we speak before we think – a perfect recipe for relationship disaster. Words, once spoken, can never be retracted – they become a permanent part of the other person's memory, or "mental-tape". And, if these words are emotionally-damaging – the relationship can take a direct hit.

Let's now examine the second pair: mind and emotions – which do you think is the superior-most – who is the boss? Does mind dictate emotions, or does emotions override the mind, or do they operate independent of each other, or are they really one and the same thing? Mind is supposed to be the boss – guiding and dictating all the other entities – but, somehow, I think that our feelings and emotions overrule our thinking – especially when it comes to our relationship issues.

The lesson that I am trying to derive from this unscientific discussion is that our relationships should not be dictated by our feelings and emotions, or by our bodily functions. Rather, our mind should be the central authority – to think and control the functioning of all other entities.

Medium of Connecting: The Speech

We all know that how and what we say to each other during the course of our interactions can become instrumental in spoiling our relationships. Actually, the situation is more complex than that. It is not only what we say that causes relationship discord, but it is also what interpretation the other person derives from what we say that becomes even more of a factor causing relationship problems. Surely, if we say something bad or wrong or unwarranted, it would, obviously, create dissensions. But, most often, even when the content of our speech is totally well intentioned, we still end up in a relationship brawl. And I am sure you can recall many scenarios of your own relationship life where such a dilemma has happened – where you said something to your spouse or relative in absolute honesty and with perfectly good intentions, but the other person got angry with you on what you said. And you were totally bewildered and puzzled as to what has happened and you are simply saying to yourself: what did I do – where did I go wrong? According to you, you did not say anything wrong, but unfortunately, not according to the other and how the other construed the intent of your message.

So, the question is: why does this happen – why does the other person make faulty interpretations or judgments of your good-intentioned message. Well, here are some plausible explanations:

- Perhaps the content of your message, itself, however good or well intentioned, was not in conformity with the thinking or expectation of the other person.

- Perhaps it was not the time and place for the message.
- Perhaps the other person was not in the state of mind, at that point in time, to be happily receptive to your message. This is something very important to note — that each person has swings of mood and a right message can be interpreted as wrong if the mood is not right or not conducive to the situation or to the nature of the message. And I am sure that you would have experienced occasions when you said something to your spouse, and it was taken to be derogatory and sarcastic, even when the same message, having been said many times before, was happily accepted.
- Perhaps your bodily gestures that accompanied your speech — or the tone of your message — were not in line with the good intentions of your message. And, by the way, you should know that the intentions — good or bad — of your message are only known to you — they are not visible or fully known to the other. Your gestures and mannerisms might have exhibited sarcasm or rudeness, and were irritable. For example, you say something good, but you can roll your eyes or shrug your shoulders in such a way that your verbal message, however good-intentioned, may provide a bad, misleading, wrongful, or deceptive impression — at least vis-à-vis the understanding of the other person.
- Perhaps, and most importantly, the other person's "mental-tape" about you is completely full of animosity towards you and consequently, whatever you may say — good or bad — is taken in the wrong perspective — whether it is actually wrong or right. The other person has a lot of pent-up feelings against you and therefore, whatever is coming from you is bad irrespective.
- And lastly, perhaps the other person's own personality make-up is so negativistic in outlook that he/she will always distort the meanings of your message — or anybody's message, for that matter — and would manifest the feelings that the message has bad intentions.

On the other end of the spectrum, it is also important to keep in mind that if your message does have bad intentions then all of the arguments we have listed apply to you also. That means — that you have a negative attitude — that you have built-in feelings of animosity against the other — that your own personality make-up is unhealthy.

Reiterating, I wish to say a bit more about the two important issues of "misunderstandings" and "misinterpretations" because they are, in my view, the most recurring and most damaging entities that plague our day-to-day relationship harmony. Misunderstandings can happen independently, or they can arise out of misinterpretations. Being the most commonly-occurring behavioral modes of our routine interactions, they inflict heavy, but silent, damage on our feelings and emotions – causing irritability, anger, and frustration – that seriously affects the accumulation of impressions about the other on our tapes. If you sincerely want to create a happy and harmonious relationship, then misunderstandings have virtually no place in this scenario. Misinterpretations, on the other hand, are generally a by-product of your own maladjusted personality and inappropriate pent-up feelings – and unless you rectify that and clear your mind of those unwanted misgivings, you can never hope to realize permanent relationship harmony and bliss.

Modes of Behavior

Next, let's examine the modes of behavior that exert an impact on our relationship interactions. Basically, there are three modes of connecting (see schematic below), which accompany our speech and behavior – that collectively create a total picture of how we connect to others during the course of our interactions:

- Positive behavioral mode
- Negative behavioral mode
- Neutral behavioral mode

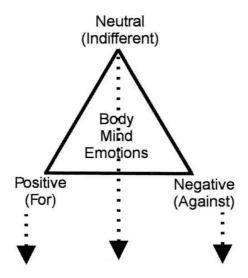

Supportive   Distant   Critical
Receptive   Disinterested   Defensive
Appreciative   Dispassionate   Cunning
Respectful   Indifferent   Sneaky
Open-minded   Sitting on the fence Cold
Passionate   Colorless   Fault-failing
Sympathetic   Impressionless   Scornful
Understanding   Self-centered   Disrespectful
Compassionate   Selfish   Hostile
Kind   Unfriendly   Disapproving
Warm   Impersonal   Arrogant
Caring   Cool   Distant

Figure 2 - Modes of Behavior

These behavioral modes, when they accompany your speech and other bodily gestures during your interactions and confrontations, they can convey a specific message that triggers a response in the other person on the intentions of your message. And that determines how the other person interprets these cues and how he/she will perceive your intentions, which in turn determines what happens in the relationship.

Modes of Connecting

Besides the positive and negative modes, I am also including the "neutral" mode because this can be equally damaging to the relationships. The neutral mode can manifest its influence in the following two ways:

- First, the other person can even get angry on your silence – on your not saying anything – because that is associated with indifference, selfishness, distance, or unfriendliness. Silence may also signify that you are hiding something, which sends a message of mistrust to the other.
- Second, if in your silence mode, your accompanying bodily gestures and behavioral attitude manifests a wrong impression to the other person – that can also create dissensions.

The Action

Finally, the action that you might pursue during, or in conjunction with, a confrontational situation may also cause a relationship brawl. A few examples of possible actions: you may have insulted your spouse or your brother-in-law in front of others; you may have betrayed your spouse's trust; you may have been unduly harsh on your child; or any such action. All these actions, whatever their nature or intensity, can leave an emotional scar on the person – a scar that never gets filled – a scar that goes into the other person's permanent mental records. Actions are especially damaging if they are loaded with emotions. Therefore, besides what you say and how you behave, your accompanying actions can exert an equally potent impact on your relationships.

The Solution – The Person

Now we come to the final stage of our new perspective. Moving from paradigm to paradigm, we have arrived at the conclusion that it is "you" – the "person" – who is responsible for all that happens in the relationship. Isn't it funny – didn't we know that anyway. Yes, but we were always busy dealing with the mediums through which a person behaves, and never the person himself. Well then, now that we are ready to focus our attention on the "person", the obvious questions to ask are:
- Who and what is this "person" that we are talking about?
- What makes this "person" the unique person?
- How do we bring about mid-course corrections into this "person"?

The Person We Are

Basically, a person is a sum total of the following three entities – at least, vis-à-vis relationship issues:

- Mind
- Feelings and emotions
- Personality make-up

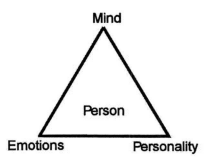

Figure 3 - The Three Entities of a Person

Personality is what makes us what we are, and each one of us has a distinctly unique personality. Mind is the controlling agent – or at least it is supposed to be our guide and mentor. Feelings and emotions are things that interject between what the mind says we should do and what the personality allows us to do. Ideally, our thinking mind is, or should, indeed, be the controlling authority – controlling and dictating our feelings and emotions, and shaping and reshaping our personality. But unfortunately, that's not what happens in reality. Our life – our actions – our behavior – they are all largely dictated by our feelings and emotions – which is a pity because that is precisely the root-cause of our relationship disharmony. As a matter of fact, it's a kind of vicious circle – our thinking mind, and feelings and emotions shape our personality and, when that is done, our personality influences our thinking, feelings, and emotions. And all of these three entities – thinking mind, emotions and feelings, and personality – put together, ultimately influences the entities of our behavior – that is what makes us "us".

Whether it's our evolutionary drawback or whether it is the way we are, typically we humans are "feelings and emotions" machines. Our uncontrolled emotionality keeps us constantly hyped-up in the mode of "reacting", rather than "responding" or "submitting" – and this keeps our self-conscious emotional-sensitivity level high. In this state, it is as if we are continuously sitting on the virtual edge of ego-sensitivity – where a single tilt of unwanted or unperceived act of bad behavior can throw us off-balance. And when that happens, we go into the self-dignity-safeguard-survival-mode and we are ready and armed to fight back to defend our dignity and ego – even when a fight is neither warranted nor appropriate. Such a state of wrongful preparedness of "reacting" and "defending" – when enacted repetitively over and over again over time – generates a continuous build-up of more anger and antagonism. This build-up, in the form of emotional outbursts, causes dissentions in relationship interactions and, this ultimately leads to bad behavior and broken relationships. On top of it, of course, some of our dominant personality characteristics – such as aggressiveness, anger, and immaturity – join hands with our feelings and emotions to create a deadly potent mix for relationships.

What Makes Us "Us"

Mind, feelings, and emotions are very elusive entities – they don't lend themselves to easy understanding and control. Therefore, in the final analysis – what makes us "us" is our total personality make-up. Fortunately, this is good news because personality characteristics are something over which we can exercise our control and make positive changes. So, it is our personality characteristics that collectively gives us a profile – makes us the person we are – impacts our thinking – makes us behave the way we do – which impacts our relationships. Therefore, backtracking, we can see that to improve our relationships, we have to improve they way we behave and act and to improve that, we have to improve upon the set of personality characteristics that impact our behavior.

What you need to do is look at the whole "you" – understand what makes you "you" – what personality factors impact to make you what you are – and then try to change and amend those personality-behavioral factors one by one to create a new "you" – one that will be permanently at peace to create harmonious relationships, once and for all – permanently.

The next question, therefore, is: What are those personality characteristics that impinge upon our behavior and make us behave the way we do. There are a very large number of personality characteristics that shape our thinking and give us a specific profile – a persona. In this book, I am including the following twelve behavioral-personality factors, which I think exert the most profound influence on our person – and hence, on our relationships:

1. Silent Stress
2. Mental-Tape
3. Variety
4. Righteousness
5. Ego
6. Aggressiveness
7. Maturity
8. Thinking
9. Anger
10. Fantasy
11. Expectations
12. Fulfilment

For each of these characteristics, we need to understand the following:

- What is our total profile vis-à-vis their collective impact?
- How does it impact our behavior?
- How do we bring about requisite personality changes?

This now brings us to a level of understanding where we can conceptualise what is involved in the process of relationships. We are a product of our personality – our personality gives us a persona – which makes us the "person" we are. This influences our behavior, by virtue of which we behave and act in a certain way in our relationship interplay and which ultimately determines the state of health of our relationships. Therefore, to make our relationships harmonious, we need to improve upon those characteristics of our personality that impinge upon our behavior.

Re-Inventing the Person

Once you have completed the cycle of this model – and you have amended the requisite personality characteristics that impinge upon your behavior – you are now ready for the final step – rejuvenating and reinventing the "new you". This involves two processes: "Awakening" and "Inner-Evolution".

Awakening is a process that involves waking-up your psyche to achieve a conscious-level awareness of the "self". Basically, it involves the following three steps:

- The Awareness: Knowing what you are and how you behave
- The Acceptance: Accepting your shortcomings
- The Passion: Desire and determination to enhance your "self"

Inner-Evolution immediately follows the Awakening. With a total awareness of the "self" and of the "other", you now go into the introspective thinking mode to improve your behavior and hence your relationship. Inner-Evolution involves the following three steps:

- Knowing the self
- Knowing the other
- Passion for harmony

Both these processes, the Awakening and the Inner-Evolution, shall be further elaborated later in section 4.

5
THE PROCESS OF LIFE

"How long can you postpone happiness with promises;
Why tomorrow – why not today."

How does the process of relationships span our life – at what stage, what type of problems occur, and why. This is something very important to understand in order to optimally utilize our new thoughts to generate and sustain relationship harmony. To explain that, I would like to present a unique overview of the total span of our life – but in a rather interesting and amusing manner. To do that, I am going to compartmentalize the span of our life into the following three broad phases:

- Phase 1: The Breakfast Phase: from birth to about 25 years
- Phase 2: The Lunch Phase: roughly between 25 to 55 years
- Phase 3: The Dinner Phase: beyond 55

This, of course, is a very rudimentary compartmentalization of the life span, but it is good enough to generate an interesting dialogue.

The Breakfast Phase

At "Breakfast" time, we are hungry – we are in the mode of making relationships, not breaking them. We are, generally, busy in three things:

- Attempting to gain "awareness" of the self, and of the self in relation to others.
- Fighting to establish our unique "identity".
- Developing our unique "personality".

In this phase, we do make some friends and business relationships, and possibly marital ones as well – but in general, most of our relationships are that of our relatives, which we inherit as a by-product of our birth, and which are already ready-made for us. We live into these relationships, enjoy, and solidify our bonds. At the same time, these relationships provide us a baseboard to develop our "person" – our "personality". Breakfast is, therefore, a period of making relationships – not breaking them – because there is nothing to break. So this phase has very few relationship problems, except for a few minor discordant annoyances with parents and relatives.

But it is also in this phase where we learn and do things, and become the person we are – and that is what influences our life and relationships in the next two phases. We begin, in this phase, to become aware of our feelings and emotions and our sense of ego and self-esteem. We begin to develop our thinking mind, our feelings of empathy for others, and our sense of maturity and responsibility. In short, this is where we develop our unique "personality". This is also where we begin the process of generating the "mental-tape" – of forming our opinions and impressions about others.

So, if in this phase, we can bring about the awareness of who we are, how we behave and act, and how can we modify our behavior, then we can expect to have smooth sailing in our relationships in the next two phases. And making changes to your person-personality is easier in this phase because you are just beginning to establish the self and, with very little effort, you can establish the self the way you want to – good or bad. Once the personality traits become hardened over time and become an unchangeable, integral part of "you", you may find it difficult to make any changes later in life – and that's where disappointments occur, at a later stage, when relationships go up and down.

The Lunch Phase

By the time we enter the "Lunch" phase, we have the following feelings about ourselves:

- We have a clear awareness of the self – "me" as a distinct entity.
- We have almost established a basic personality profile for ourselves.
- We are well established in the relationships that we inherited by virtue of birth.
- We have established, or are in the process of establishing, marital and other business and social relationships.

Let's now examine what transpires in our relationships in this phase, especially with regard to our main focus – the core marital relationship. Let me make a strong, but almost true, statement right here: while the Lunch phase is the beginning of the makings of this new relationship, it is also, unfortunately, the beginning of its breakings. Typically, most of the marital relationships are made and broken in the Lunch phase. The peak breaking point of this relationship is, normally, in the first five to seven years after marriage. Why does that happen? Basically, as per my new perspective, breakings happen in this phase because of "personality" differences. Personality make-up is the only new thing we have imported and added on to us between the Breakfast phase and the Lunch phase. At Breakfast time, we generate personality – at Lunch time, we use this personality to interact and react. And how the marital relationship will grow and flourish depends on how the two personalities have evolved during the Breakfast phase, and how compatible they are or can be made in the Lunch phase.

Having said that, I would like to remind you that the breakings rarely occur because of a single incidence or factor – it is always the result of a multitude of factors and confrontations put together. And also that, the breakings just don't happen out of the blue – like a big surprise one fine morning – it is the outcome of a slow degenerative process of a build-up of antagonistic feelings, layer-by-layer, slowly over time. And when they reach their boiling point, they burst open at the marital seam. Speaking about the impact of personality, there are, indeed, many personality factors that affect our relationships – individually as well as collectively – such as ego, aggressiveness, anger, maturity, hostility, fulfillment, etc. Most of this shall be elaborated as we go along the book, but meanwhile, let me examine just one characteristic – that of "aggressiveness" – which I think exerts the greatest impact on the breakings of relationships in the Lunch phase.

Generally, it's a well-known fact that men are relatively more aggressive than women – nothing good or bad, right or wrong – just the way we are. Of course, it doesn't mean that women are not aggressive as well. In fact, men are more ego-sensitive aggressive, while women are more feelings-sensitive aggressive. And, in my view, most of the relationship problems that occur in the Lunch phase are because of men's over-aggressive and overbearing behavior. This means that the development of personality in the Breakfast phase is, perhaps, different for both sexes. If that is so, then why don't we notice this "aggressiveness" before marriage? The answer is simple – at the time of the marriage vows, or the time preceding the vows, both parties are emotionally charged with the desire to consummate the relationship. As such, therefore, our analytical lenses are generally fogged up with our blinding desires and emotional feelings, and they don't allow us to know the real and true extent and nature of each other's personality. It is only when the honeymoon is over, that reality starts dawning and the true personality colors, which, of course, were inherently there all the time but were not evident, now come into the visible forefront. With the reality in front of us, we begin to abhor and detest each other's overbearing and aggressive behavior, and slowly, the relationship starts deteriorating.

The Dinner Phase

"Dinner" time has arrived, and here you look back at the Lunch and Breakfast phases, and have the following feelings:

- Feelings of love, happiness, companionship, fulfillment; or
- Feelings of anger, repentance, and hopelessness

Normally, relationships should not break in this phase because it's not worth it, and also, this is when we need each other's companionship the most. But unfortunately, that's not the case – many a relationships do end up breaking up in the Dinner phase, or if they don't physically break, they end up suffering from "silent separations". In fact, my observation tells me that a "very large" number of relationships go into "silent separations" in this phase. So much so that I am inclined to rename the "Dinner phase" as the "silent separations phase". There are a lot of couples that I know of who are leading a life of togetherness, physically – but they are lost to each other mentally. They suffer in silence – with anger and frustration – because they can't break the relationship for one reason or another, and they also don't want to stay in the relationship either.

Why does this happen? Once again, the answer lies in the mental-tape effect. The lifelong tape of pent-up feelings is totally full – there is virtually no love left between the couple. There is a silent distance between them. They are merely the walking, talking, sulking strangers to each other. So who is to blame? For the Lunch phase – I placed the blame on men more than women, but unfortunately, for the Dinner phase, the blame seems to be leaning towards women. Men are surely more aggressive in the Lunch phase – a trait that becomes instrumental in breakdowns – but men become more mellow and sublime in the Dinner phase. They have a greater desire and need for companionship in this phase. Women, on the other hand, tend to become more aggressive in the Dinner phase – picking up where men have left off, and in some cases getting even with men. More specifically, women go through the following regimen:

- They have spent too many years in silence, in a not-so-happy relationship, with men being overly aggressive and overly aloof, and they have tolerated the relationship for one reason or another – but no more.
- They feel they have suffered enough – and they are angry.
- They feel trapped and suffocated – they want to become free and independent.

With this state of mind, many women even tend to dig up the past – the old graves of discontent – and the mental-tape is replayed, incidence-by-incidence, and the women want the men to account for every incidence and justify it. The woman wants to get even with her man – to do unto him what he did unto her in the Lunch phase.

What is the end result of all this? The relationship either goes into silent separations, or it breaks. If it breaks, she's got her independence – right? Wrong. Having gotten her independence, she is even more miserable because she has lost a partner in this old age, when she really needs one. And when she wakes up to the fact, it's too late – the husband is either gone or dead and the reality of loneliness steps in. And now, perhaps she is repentant.

What a relationship? And what a strange melodrama? The first half of our life we spend in bickering and fighting – and the second half in vengeance. The first half – the man does bad things, the second half – the woman. Tit for tat. The end result – a whole life gone into a bad relationship – a whole life wasted – and life ends – the only life that we get. Surely that's not the purpose of life. And what a strange paradox – we abhor the other person when he is alive – and we cry for him when he is dead.

In conclusion, I think this discussion should provide some useful information on what transpires in our relationships in various stages of our life, which can guide us to channel our relationship more effectively towards greater harmony.

SECTION 3
JOURNEY INTO THE UNKNOWN
THE REASON

6
THE PERSON – THE PERSONALITY
– THE PERSONA

"The world is a mirror image of your own thinking;
It's happy, if you are happy;
It's miserable, if you are miserable."

All through our previous discussion, we reinforced our new realization that behind all of our relationship problems is a "person" – a "personality" – the generator of the mediums of speech and behavior, which is the real causing agent of the relationship discord. It is, therefore, time that we discuss that person, and find out what personality characteristics impact and shape that person. As such, the whole of section 3 is devoted to understanding these personality traits to see how they shape our being.

The Person

What is a person? In terms of relationships, a person is known by the personality profile he has, which is, of course, a collective by-product of many diverse factors. In common language, this profile is what we call a person's nature, a mirror of the mode of his behavior. How does a person acquire this nature? Of all the factors that make up what we call our "nature", some factors are acquired through birth, while others through the process of learning and interacting with the society we live in. I have chosen twelve important characteristics of personality, which I think exert the most influence on the person's profile, and make him the person he is, and these are elaborated in this section. For each of these factors, we need to examine the following:

- How does the characteristic impact our life and relationship?
- How do we assess the level and extent of the impact?
- How do we improve upon our total profile to enhance our relationship?

Remember, there is no one single factor that bears such a phenomenal impact on the person's profile that it becomes instrumental in destroying a relationship. Each factor brings in a certain behavioral oddity and idiosyncrasy in the person's profile – and the collective impact of all such oddities, that is the total profile of the person, is what causes irritability in the relationship interactions. The daily annoyances that occur from these behavioral oddities then cause anger and discomfort in the relationship, and these accumulate over time to cause a feeling of antagonism and disgust, leading to a breakdown in the relationship. Therefore, what we need to understand is: what is the impact of each factor, what is the collective impact of all factors on our profile, and how this affects our behavior. Briefly then, we need to decipher the person's personality profile from which we can see what changes must be made to make the person more conciliatory in creating relationship harmony. How do we study this profile? It is generally done through the persona – the outside window of the personality profile – through which we can find out what the person is like. What is a persona? Personas are faces and facades that we carry for different interactive situations of life and living. Basically, a person has two types of personas:

- Inside- persona
- Outside- persona

The outside persona is what the person portrays to the world through the outside window. The inside persona is what a person really is from the inside. In studying the profile of a person, what we really need to examine is his inside persona. But that's not possible because the inside persona is hidden inside the person and we can't get to it. The only thing we can get to is his outside persona, but then that can be very misleading. The reason is very simple – a person can have thousands of outside personas – one for every new situation he/she encounters. For example, you have one persona when you go into a church, another one when you are out of it – one facade when you speak to the boss, another one when you speak to your subordinate – one face when you speak to your spouse, another one when you speak to your child.

Another difficulty with the outside persona is that you can borrow, wear, and mimic other people's personas as well. That is, you can pose as somebody that you are actually not. When you get into the habit of wearing different masks – personas – we don't know who you are, and we can't trust you – your profile is untrustworthy. This means that we have no use for the outside persona, even when that is the only one we can see and behold.

In short, it is really the "inside- persona" that is of any value to us. But as we said earlier, the inside-persona is an elusive entity, because it is a by-product of our thinking mind, feelings and emotions, and personality traits. And the situation becomes even more complex because feelings and emotions don't lend themselves to easy understanding. So what do we do? The only option we have is to study all of the person's personality traits, and then interact with him at the conscious level of his psyche to get a good picture of the inside profile.

So, here is our final challenge! In the next eleven chapters, I have described the most important personality factors that impinge upon our person – persona – to make us the person we are, and to make us behave the way we do. Our challenge, therefore, is to study them carefully, collate our findings in the context of our own personality, and get a true picture of our inside-persona. Then we should see how our "personality profile" affects our relationships, and accordingly try to make source-level changes to amend our person in order to create a new person – one who would always endeavour to maintain permanent relationship harmony.

7
SILENT STRESS

"If you use the word "sorry" any more than three times
for the same mistake with the same person,
you need to re-evaluate your behavioral wisdom."

Before I begin to examine those important personality traits that influence our behavior, I would like to first highlight a more non-specific and general aspect of our personality, which exerts tremendous influence on our day-to-day relationship interactions. This relates to our general disposition to stress and tension and the overall stressful profile that we carry as a result.

A large majority of people carry with them, constantly at all times, a kind of stressful profile and persona which signifies or at least gives the impression that they are uptight or angry. One gets the feeling that they are not approachable, and as such, it doesn't give their relationships a fair chance at harmonization and happiness. You can see these people's outside persona and easily infer that they are full of ego-pride, anger, and tension. It's a very common disease, and it may be a by-product of either some of the personality characteristics, such as aggressiveness, a righteousness syndrome, expectations, fulfillment, modes of thinking, etc., or it may be the result of personal and work related life-pressures. Let's look at the general characteristics of the person bearing the silent stress syndrome:

- He is very uptight — very tense inside, even when he may not show it.
- He is very ego-sensitive — always sitting on the virtual edge of the emotional cliff, wherefrom he can easily fall off with just a puff of unwanted behavior.
- His thinking is generally negativistic, and the conscious-level thinking person inside him is always looking for opportunities to derive wrong meanings and interpretations of life situations.

- He would never allow any discussion of his state of "silent stress", nor would he welcome any advice on that because his arrogant ego would never let him do so.

The silent stress profile is problematic because many people who have this disease don't even know that they have it; or even if they know that they have it, they would never admit or accept the fact that they are stressed. So as such, amending a person with this syndrome becomes rather difficult unless he is willing to accept the state of his being and is open to suggestions for the improvement of his modes of thinking.

Stress and Relationships

Although I am not discussing the subject of stress here, I would like to say a few general words about stress as a personality weakness factor that affects our behavior. What is stress? Stress is that "vague sense of concentration, tension, and anxiety inside us that keeps us emotionally uptight and hyped-up continuously in a state of general imbalance." Following are some important things to remember about stress:

- Stress is not a mechanical tool or entity – it is a mental disposition, which has to do with you – the person.
- Stress is not lying in wait around the corner to grab you when you pass by, nor can anybody inject stress into your body. You create stress yourself – either because of undesirable external situations, or through your own negativistic mental thinking and hypothetical imagery. In any case, you are the one who creates stress – it is inside you and affects your behavior, and therefore, you are the one who has to eliminate it. You have to ask your mind not to generate hypothetical situations that create stress, as well not to let extrinsic situations force stress upon you. Train your mind to disown what is not yours – "stress".

If you are constantly living with this built-in conscious-level stressful thinking, you will manifest a persona of anger and ego-arrogance, which displays the impression that you are unapproachable, and this makes it difficult for others to know whether you would like to maintain the relationship or not. Even when you may have good intentions and you do wish to maintain a good relationship, your stressful persona inadvertently ends up inflicting emotional damage – both on you as well as on others.

Other people get hurt because they love you and want to create a long-lasting happy relationship, but they can't because they don't get any positive vibrations from you. And in terms of damage to your own self – your staying in that constant mode of hyped-up anger and stressfulness can bring about all sorts of health problems associated with stress.

The basic difficulty with people suffering from silent stress syndrome is that they are very edgy and ego-sensitive – they don't accept any criticism of their mode of behavior, nor would they accept any advice, even when they need it. So, the end result is that they continue living in that state of mind and continue hurting their otherwise good relationships.

The proceeding eleven chapters in this section would highlight some of the factors that cause stress and would also offer some viable solutions to the problem. Irrespective of whatever you may do, you need to understand, right in the beginning, that you have to get rid of this unwanted extra baggage of silent stress yourself if you have any desire to bring happiness into your relationships.

8
MENTAL TAPE

"Think small – and you will always remain small;
Think big – and you will blossom gracefully."

With this chapter, we now begin with the first of a series of important behavioral-personality factors that profoundly impact the way we behave and act in relationships, and which become instrumental in determining the harmony of our relationships. The basic framework of my idea of "mental-tape" may not be totally new, but the mode of presentation is absolutely unique, and I am sure that you would find it interesting and informative, and as well, it will serve as a good reference point in your daily relationship interplay.

Generation of the Mental Tape

What is a mental-tape and how is it generated?

A "mental-tape" is a storehouse of our perceptions, images, impressions, and feelings about the other person – a total profile of the other person "as we see it". It is how we see and feel about the other person – the type of personality he/she has and the way he/she behaves. It is not always as how the other person actually is; it is simply our perceptions about the other.

How is this tape generated? During the course of our life, we meet people and establish relationships and associations of varying degrees and intensities. Some relationships are, indeed, self-established by virtue of our birth, while others we establish ourselves over the course of our life. For each person with whom we have a relationship, of whatever nature and intensity, I believe that we set up a "mental-tape" – audio or video, whatever you may like to call it – and we store the tape in our memory.

Thus, we have a tape for our spouse, a tape for our mother, father, for each child, for each of our relatives, for each of our friends and associates, and so on. We therefore have thousands of tapes in our head, one for each of the people we know.

The starting point of the tape is the initial interaction with the person, the first encounter. Whatever happens during this interaction, a message is recorded on the tape about what we think the other person is like. This message is our impression about the other person, and these impressions and opinions are the result of what transpired during the interaction, that is, how the other person reacted, how his/her behavior and attitude were, what he/she said, etc. All in all, it is a stepping-stone to establishing our perception of the other person's total personality profile "as we see it".

Like this, the tape then gets filled up, step-by-step, over time. As we go along in life, we keep adding more and more material on the tape, and keep adding more new tapes as we go along meeting more new people. These recorded messages on the tape become a permanent record of the person in our memory. Most of the important messages stay permanently on the tape – however, some messages and images, arising out of incidences that are of no particular significance or consequence to us, may get deleted, automatically, from the tape over time. Incidences that are highly charged with feelings and emotions, or anything that hurts our feelings and upsets our emotional balance, however, never ever get deleted – they are stone carved on the tape – they are a permanent, non-erasable entity.

Typically, that is the process by which we generate the mental-tape, or perhaps, that should be or should have been the only way of its generation – but unfortunately, that is not the case. It was during the course of my research that I observed several other different behavioral modalities, which indicated to me that there are a number of other ways in which the tape can be generated and the perceptions on it utilized as they are, during the relationship interplay. As a minimum, there are at least the following five different ways in which you can generate the tape:

1. The first one is the normal process that I have outlined above, where you generate impressions and perceptions about the other person from the way the person behaves with you during the direct one-to-one interaction, that is, his modes of speech, behavior, and actions.

2. You may also form opinions about the other from the opinions of other people about the person. As I pointed out in an earlier

section, your own nephew doesn't like you very much just because his father doesn't like you. So your nephew has formed antagonistic feelings for you on his tape about you, even when you two have never interacted directly with each other to any significant extent.

3. At times, you don't even need direct interaction or confrontation with the other person, or even someone else's opinions, to generate a mental-tape of impressions – you may generate a feeling of anger and antagonism simply by your own mental imagery, because you don't like the other person – a case of a mismatch of personality chemistry with the other person. For example, you don't like your neighbour's wife because she is too aggressive.

4. Another bad scenario – maybe you have your own unresolved emotional issues and your own anger and unhappiness is projected onto the other, creating a set of impressions that really reflect your own unhappiness, and not what the other person actually is. And this can happen even when the other person has never behaved badly with you to any extent.

5. Finally, the worst-case scenario – the tape may simply be a reflection of your own negativistic mind-set. Perhaps, in general, you are a negative person, an introverted person with a negativistic mindset, and you have a tendency to behave badly and negatively with everyone you interact with, irrespective of what others say or do.

Impact of Mental Tape on Relationships

Let's now examine how the mental-tape phenomenon affects our relationships. I believe that the health of our relationships is not only impacted by what we say to each other or how we behave with each other or what personality profile we have, but it is also influenced by the nature and intensity of the built-up impressions on the tape that we have for the other person, and, more importantly, the way the impressions were generated on the tape in the first place. This is what I call the "mental-tape effect". Our interaction with others is almost completely dictated by the built-up impressions about the other on our mental tape. In fact, the mental-tape almost completely influences our behavior with others.

Relationship interactions through the modes of built-up perceptions are the main impediment in the way of achieving relationship harmony.

If the impressions on the tape are good, you feel happy interacting with the person – you are receptive, open, compassionate, and nice to each other. If, on the other hand, the impressions are not so good, you feel agitated inside during the interaction.

How does the tape process work? When we meet or interact with a person we know, or see the person coming towards us, we take out the person's tape and start playing it. Two things can happen: our conversation will be almost totally influenced by the built-up impressions we have about the person on the tape; and we may also make minor additions or deletions in accordance with what transpires during that interaction and what interpretations we draw of the other's attitude and actions.

To elucidate – let's recount a familiar scenario. You see John coming towards you, and you don't like John very much. You say to yourself: "Oh! God – not him again." Can you now realize what has transpired here – poor John hasn't even reached near you – he hasn't said anything to you yet – but you took out John's tape and started playing it, pre-emptively. You are reacting to John, not from what he is or what he is gong to say to you, but from the built-up impressions and messages that you have about him on the tape.

This is my "mental-tape" theory.

The basic problem with the tape affect is that the impressions on the tape are not only the result of what the other said to you or how he behaved with you, it is what interpretations you drew out of what he said. Unfortunately, your own interpretation of what the other said is normally not the same as the intent of what the other said, and it may or may not be the right interpretation either. I am sure you can recount hundreds of scenarios of your own where you said something to somebody in all honesty, but the other misconstrued it as something else – something unacceptable – and the person got angry with you. And you were totally baffled as to what has happened, because according to you, you did not say anything wrong or did not mean anything bad. So, you see, it is not only what you say that goes on the other person's tape, it is also what interpretations the other makes of what you say or do that also gets registered on the tape.

Consequently, with the tape "affect" interjecting at every step of the interactive interplay, the relationship never gets a fair and independent chance at blooming and prospering – it is always coloured by the already-built-up impressions about the other person. When the tape for the other is full with bad feelings, you can become completely obnoxious to the other person. You don't like anything that he says – in fact you are always ready to negate him.

Although trivial and meaningless things that you say to each other on a daily basis should not and need not go on the tape, unfortunately, that's where the whole dilemma lies – because what you say may be trivial according to you, but you don't know how the other person is interpreting it and what he/she is putting on the tape.

Many marital relationships suffer because of this phenomenon. Husband and wife, and relatives and friends keep saying things to each other – out of love or as a joke – not knowing how each one is taking it and what interpretations each one is making of those unintentional and innocent gestures and sayings. Also you don't know how and what each one is registering on the tape, and what and how the accumulation of impressions is happening. Over time, the antagonism and anger builds up – the tape gets full – and there is a huge reservoir of pent-up feelings of anger and hostility. Sometimes, that hostility and anger is visible, but most often it is hidden inside – dormant – but ready to burst out anytime. And the worst part is that many a times you may not even know about the existence of either the tape or the accumulated feelings on the tape that the other person has, because according to you, you have never ever said anything bad or wrong. When there is no more room left on the tape, then a single confrontational incidence, of any intensity, can trigger the outburst of that accumulated reservoir of emotional feelings, and the sleeping volcano can burst out with a big bang. The relationship takes a direct hit, and it either goes into a spasm of silent separations, or it may lead up to separation or divorce.

In line with this, let me tell you something utterly unique – something that you may have never contemplated before – about the interplay of mental-tape and marital-relationship breakdown. When a marital relationship breaks down and ends up in a separation or divorce, the parties are ready, after a reasonable cooling-off period, to start building new relationships. They start looking for a new mate to carry on the process of companionship – an unavoidably essential part of life and living. Very soon, voila! They find someone – someone that they think is very much better than their previous mate that they divorced. Now they think they have really found the right one – the most compatible one, and consequently, they establish the relationship once more.

Nothing wrong with the process or the feelings, and I hope it works, but unfortunately, some of these people are not aware of my mental-tape theory. What they don't know is that the other new mate seems more suitable than any mate they had before, simply because at the moment their tapes for each other are empty, there is nothing on their tapes of any concern. What they also don't understand is that very soon they will create a new tape for each other, and the tape will start its journey of getting filled up with feelings and emotions for each other. Of course, the tape can have good things also, and many a times that is the case or I hope that is the case, but there is always the possibility that the tape can once again be filled up with antagonistic feelings, and all that depends on your personality make-up. And if these tapes end up being completely filled up with antagonistic feelings, then once again the relationship can go into silent separations or can even lead to another break-up.

So you can see my point – how people's tapes can play such a damaging emotional game with their relationships. The tape gets filled up – find a new partner with an empty tape – the new partner's tape again gets filled up – find another new partner with an empty tape – and so on and so forth – the vicious circle never ends.

The solution does not lie in continuously looking for partners with empty tapes, one after the other, and get sucked into misleading mental imagery. The solution lies in what I annotate as "emptying the tape" – continuously – with your existing partner.

Before I close my discussion, I want to present another scenario, in line with the above discussion. There is another unique thought in my mind – that perhaps, marital infidelity is also another aspect where the tape affect plays a significant role. Although, in the case of infidelity, there may be a multitude of factors at play, perhaps people become attracted to other people, out of their own marriage, simply because their own tapes are full of antagonistic feelings for their own spouses, and their tapes are empty with others they meet. And since empty tapes are more palatable than tapes full of antagonistic feelings, it becomes an easy and vulnerable factor that can initiate and lead into a relationship of infidelity, outside the marital bonds.

In closing, I want to set the facts right and say that: although there are reasonably plausible situations where a separation/divorce becomes imminent, yet we should keep in mind the power of the mental-tape-affect and control the situation with utmost maturity and judiciousness. The tape has profound impact on our relationships. If there is a lesson we can learn, it is this: never ever underestimate the power of the little things that you say to each other, you have no idea how they are being interpreted by the other person, and how the person is registering and accumulating those impressions and feelings on the tape. Each little incidence or skirmish may have very little strength and force by itself, but the cumulative effect can be deadly.

Things once said are never retractable. You open your mouth once and say something bad, it will never be forgotten. It will become a permanent, non-erasable part of the other person's mental-tape, and this is especially true if what you said was loaded with emotional elements. Even if you say sorry or apologize, it doesn't matter – the damage is done. In fact, you may find that both are recorded on the other person's tape – "what you said as well as your apology".

So profoundly strong are the recordings on the tape that when you are arguing or fighting with your spouse over something, for example, you will notice that your spouse will not only limit the fight to the present issue in question, but will also try to recall and bring in other sore issues from the previous arguments, even when those may be totally unrelated to the issue on which you are presently fighting. This is the "recalling affect" of the tape. Actually, if this happens, it can also be a very powerful indication that, deep down the other person has very strong, and perhaps hidden, built-up feelings of anger and antagonism against you.

So, here is the moral of the story vis-à-vis the emotional sensitivities of the tape:

- Be aware of the other person's sensitivity threshold.
- Be sensitive to the other person's feelings and emotions.
- Stop the habit of hoarding up your feelings.
- Keep emptying the tape as frequently as you keep filling it, or better, destroy the tape altogether.

This concept of the mental-tape phenomenon is the first in the series of eleven factors that I decided to elucidate in this section, to understand how these personality characteristics impart their influence on our person. As I indicated earlier, any one single factor would not have the power to destroy the relationship, but the collective impact of all the factors can exert profound influence that can lead to relationship estrangement and disharmony.

Having understood the concept, you should now check, from your own behavior, as to how you interact with others from your own preconceived impressions about them — the mental tape. When you fill the other person's tape with nothing but negative feelings, you automatically, without even realizing, close all doors to a positive interaction with the person. You are always negative to the person. Whatever the person says is wrong, irrespective. In fact, you look for opportunities to put the other down.

But this is where your maturity plays a very important role. You should always go into the introspective thinking mode and evaluate the situation, as judiciously as possible, to see if it is your own mental negative imagery that has blocked your better judgment via your tape, or is the other really as bad as he is or as you think he is.

This completes our discussion of one major factor that influences our behavior that can exert a profound effect on our relationships. Although one single factor cannot be instrumental in spoiling a relationship, it can create a large enough reservoir of bad feelings to bring the relationship to a breaking point. Like this, as you go along, study the impact of other factors, and then ultimately examine the collective impact of all factors, to get a clear view of your total profile.

Additional information and solutions for dealing with this dilemma of the tape affect shall be discussed further in section 5 of the book.

9

VARIETY

*"Flowers share their fragrance without expectations of any returns;
Share your love like a flower."*

Now I would like to consider the second behavioral-personality factor – the "variety". What do I mean by "variety"? It is a new paradigm that I am propounding – and here is what it means: God, in His infinite wisdom, has created everything and everybody "different" – in likes-dislikes, tastes, behavior, personality, etc. Also, God has given an equal right to everybody to do what they think is best. Yet despite that, we disregard this act of God and spend our whole relationship life forcing each other to behave the way we do, knowing well that everybody is different, thinks differently, and would act and behave differently. And all of this profoundly influences the health and harmony of our relationships.

Digressing for a moment – there is a funny story behind how this idea came to my mind. Somewhere in the process of thinking about these eleven behavioral-personality factors, suddenly, one day, an amusing thought struck my mind and I asked myself a question: "Are all personality traits acquired and learned, or are some God-given?" Rephrasing the question, I asked myself: "Does God have something to do with the way we are, and the way we behave?" After considerable deliberations, I came to the conclusion that the answer is – "both" – they are acquired as well as God-given. The acquired ones come to us via our lifelong living in and interacting with our society, and many of these traits can be de-acquired as well, if we make an effort. On the question of God, I argued – surely we are a creation of God, and there must be some aspects of our being and having that must have come to us with our birth – as God's gift to us. I am sure you must be saying that it is not nice to bring God into the affairs of human relationships – what has God to do with the way we behave. But, with due reverence to God – if God created us the way we are, then surely it would be worth looking into our behavior, at least for the sake of discussion, to see if God meant us the way we are.

Although we are what we are – a creation of God – which may seem to mean that our entire being, that is, our total personality, is altogether God-given. Yet, as I progressed with my search, I isolated and chose just about only two factors that I would say are the gifts of God: "variety" – discussed in this chapter, and "righteousness" – elaborated in the next chapter.

I must emphasize that my conjectures about "variety" and "righteousness" are not, by any means, unheard of before – they are a common knowledge. The only thing new about it is the way I am presenting them – in an amusing manner. And that is done with a purpose – so that they will make a lasting impression on your memory recall. For the sake of easy reference throughout the book, I am going to annotate these two gifts of God as: GG1 (God's Gift # 1: Variety) and GG2 (God's Gift # 2: Righteousness).

God's Gift # 1 (GG1): Variety

"God made everyone different."

Whether it is the human race, the animal kingdom, or plant life – every single individual of every species, irrespective of it's shape, size, color, creed, race, or sex – is different, however small or large the difference. We all look different from each other – we all think differently – we behave and act differently – our emotional reactions are different – our personalities are different – we have different tastes, likes and dislikes – we have different desires, opinions, and convictions – all in all – we are uniquely different from each other – each one of us is a unique person – a distinct entity.

A subtle point to keep in mind right here is that I am only speaking about the differences, and that has nothing to do with being better or worse, right or wrong, superior or inferior.

Elaborating GG1

GG1: Variety

The fact that we are all different is almost a commonsense reality. Not only do we think and behave differently, or have different emotional thresholds, we are even genetically different. Every single individual has a unique and different genetic blueprint. And, to prove my point, though I really don't have to because you all know that we are all different, let's consider the human body itself. If the human body is just an assemblage of spare parts, all bearing the same name and characteristic over the entire human population, then why does a transplant of one person's body parts into another person's body gets rejected by the recipient's body? Does one person's heart, for example, have different strings of feelings and emotions that only go with that person's overall body mechanism, and not with another person's body. A silly example, but a strong one to make a point – that we are all different.

The question is, that knowing well this reality that we are all different – think and behave differently – have different likes and dislikes – and that each one of us has a right to be what we are, why do we spend our whole lifetime bickering and fighting with each other over ridiculously minor and trivial things – trying to change the other to our way of thinking and behaving. Typically, it is because of the "righteousness" syndrome that I will elucidate in the next chapter – where we think that we know all – we are always right – and because of that we want the others to do what we do. But that is almost ridiculous! Just because you have self-assumed yourself as always right doesn't, in any way, mean that you are actually right. In fact, most of the people who are afflicted with this disease of self-righteousness, arrogance, and non-acceptance of other people's opinions are, in fact, generally themselves wrong. Their internal blindness, unfortunately, doesn't let them see that. And even funnier is the fact that, if you ever ask these people the question: "Do you believe that you are always right", they would categorically deny it – never ever would they accept it, even when, deep down inside them, they do uphold the stance that they are always right.

Let's consider a simple routine scenario – between my wife and myself, for example – we may have spent almost thirty years trying to change each other. She wants me to eat broccoli, and I hate it – and I want her to eat seafood, and she doesn't want to. More weird – and to strengthen her righteousness stance – she would put forth hundreds of arguments to support her claim such as, for example – the majority of people eat broccoli, or broccoli is good for you. And the funny thing is that we are still at it – going strong – trying to force each other to do what each one of us think is right or good, and nobody knows how long we will still keep doing it – though thirty years should have been enough of a time period to make us realize that we need to stop the process of trying to change each other. Silly little example – I know – but good enough to show how relationships can suffer because of the accumulated impact of even simple daily naggings and skirmishes. Our daily routine of life is full of scenarios like this where we are busy trying to point out to the other that he/she is wrong, and trying to convince the other to change to our way of doing things, because ours is the only right way.

Another trivial scenario – a number of my close relatives and friends are sore with me because they say that I am too exact, too precise, and too regimented. Their argument is that: "We are all humans – and human life doesn't have to be that exact". In my humble somnolence, I might have agreed to the stance of these people, but I don't – because of the following:

- Why should I believe that humans are not supposed to be exact when we all seek exactness, perfection, and excellence in everything we do?
- These same people who complain about my exactness would turn around and start referring to how exact and precise their own standards are, and complain about why other people can't operate with preciseness as they do. For example, they would want the paper delivery on time, they want people to honour their meeting appointments to be precisely on time, they want their services to be very precise and of excellent quality, and so on. Why do these people live by double or, perhaps, multiple standards – one for themselves, and another one for others.

Presumably, I don't think there is anything wrong with being exact and precise – do you? And more amusingly, I have never complained or disliked these people just because they are not precise, though at times I feel that I have as much right to be angry with these people because of their impreciseness, as they have with my preciseness.

In your own relationship situations, you must have encountered people who refuse to recognize GG1 (variety), and insist on demanding that you do what they think best. They won't accept that your likes and dislikes are different. Why is it so? It is simply because their arrogant ego, which makes them think that they are always right, won't allow them to accept the fact that the other is different, because for them, acceptance means "defeat" – and that's a no-no for the ego.

Let me describe to you another situation that you may never have contemplated before, at least in the format in which I am presenting. Consider the scenario of dating and marriage – the time period when a boy and a girl of marriageable age are seeking for the right partner to start their family life. I had a chance to ask many prospective potential couples: "What are you looking for in the other person?" And a large majority of the time, the answer was: "We are looking for a mate with similar tastes, and a similar thinking mind". Isn't that incredibly strange and abnormal – vis-à-vis GG1 – isn't that wishing against the will of God – who, in His infinite wisdom, created everyone with different tastes and different thinking minds.

Anyway, let's continue with the story. So this couple has now found a perfect match for each other, and they happily get married. Not even four years pass by and they start bickering about the differences in their likings, tastes, and thinking.

- I like broccoli, why don't you.
- I want to go to the movies, you want to stay home.
- I want to travel, you want to rest.
- And so on

So, what has happened? The make-believe passion of similarities, under the guile of which the union was consummated, is wearing off – the honeymoon is over – the reality is beginning to dawn – the will and act of God is emerging as the winner – the bare reality is coming to the forefront – "that we are all inherently different".

Actually let me ask you something – of the married couples you know, how many you can say with confidence that the husband and wife are totally similar in their thinking. Personally, I can't even find one couple where the likings and dislikings of the husband and wife are the same. At least ninety percent of most couple's thinking and doing is different from each other. It sounds funny! On one hand, we humans love "variety" in almost every aspect of our life and living: food, travel, household effects, work, flowers, nature, etc. – yet we don't tolerate "variety" in each other's behavior and attitude.

Turning back to the scenario of marriage and dating, indeed I was not saying that dating is not the right way to a happy matrimony or that you should not look for somebody who has similar likings and dislikings as you have. In fact, on the contrary, it is the only right way to consummate the relationship, and it is also very essential to seek compatibility before marriage. All I am emphasizing is that underneath all that, we should be consciously aware of the fact that we are all different – and we should work towards generating togetherness, with full acceptance, understanding and respect for each other's individuality.

What I am propounding is that we should consider our differences as our strength, and utilize this diversity to generate togetherness. Our relationship harmony and oneness should always be based on the unequivocal understanding that we are different from each other, and yet we want to become one. Instead of constantly brooding over our differences and keeping our relationship in perpetual limbo, we should appreciate each other's unique individuality and enjoy our diversity. Same goes for marriage. We should choose each other with a clear understanding that we are different, but also with a clear commitment that we would seek and work for togetherness out of our diversity.

In my own life, I have encountered hundreds of such friends and relatives, who just fail to accept, consciously or unconsciously, the fact that God has created everyone different. Most of these people want the world to be a mirror image of their own mind – their own thinking – their own rights and wrongs – because they think that their way of thinking is the only right way – why – because God told them so – not realizing, of course, that God told everybody so.

Let me recount another mini scenario. Steve and myself live almost next door to each other. We occasionally drive together to our friend, Robert's house, about 5 miles. There are basically three routes to go to Robert's house, all virtually equidistant. Steve drives via one route and I drive via a different one. The problem is that whenever I drive, via the route I am used to, Steve gets angry because he wants me to drive via the route he uses, insisting that his is the best of the three routes. And this meaningless confrontation seems to have no end. One day, I stopped the car on the road-side and asked Steve the following:

- I said – Steve, do you believe in God – and he said – yes.
- I said – do you see that God has created every one of us different, in every respect – he said – yes.
- And I said – then why can't I do differently than you do – why can't I have the right to do what I want to – when God has given me an independent life, as distinct from yours – why can't I drive through the route that I like.

84

- Steve agreed – but – and there is always a "but" in between – he still insisted that the route he takes is a better one.

You think the story ended there – no! For that moment in time, Steve agreed and accepted, but given a lapse of time, he again forgot GG1 (that we are different) and emphasized GG2 (that he is right).

The funny part of this game is that when you ask the other person, if God created everyone different, and that if everyone has a right to do differently or do whatever they like to, the answer would be a definite "yes". And yet these same people would forget that and would turn around to insist upon your doing what they think is right. I can recount hundreds of more such scenarios in my own relationships where the person knows that "variety" is a fact of life – accepts it – yet doesn't want to stand by it.

Sometimes I am at a loss for words, as to what to say about these people – why do they do that – why are they absolutely bent on their desire to change others to their way of doing things, even when their way of thinking is not necessarily the right one? The best I can think of is that such people have maladjusted profiles. When people don't accept the fact that every person is different – will behave differently – and has an inherent right to do so – it's bound to cause problems in relationships. Their actions can plague the relationship harmony, slowly and systematically, leading the relationship to bankruptcy, and ultimately to silent separations, or even breakdowns.

Let me now wrap up my thoughts on the subject of "variety" by giving some general guidelines that will not only apply to "Variety", but also to all types of personality factors that impinge on our behavior:

- What and how you think and perceive things is not necessarily the same as others do. It's not a matter of being right or wrong – it's a matter of being different. God, in His infinite wisdom, made each one of us different from the other – why – I don't know – but I am sure that there must be a purpose behind His grand scheme of things.
- When you expect people to do what you do, because you think you are always right – ask yourself why? If it is because God told you so, then you must also remember that everybody else thinks the same way also, and that God told the same thing, equally, to everyone else also. You are not the only smart Alex

in the world, everyone else is also equally right and smart, if not more smarter than you. In fact, it is your own arrogance that impedes your better judgment and doesn't let you appreciate the individuality of each person. Personally, I think that arrogance is the first sign of a lack of intellectual confidence.

- A relationship is simply a matter of give and take – you cannot only take – take – take – and expect the relationship to flourish – you have to give also, almost as equally as you take, and this means respect for each other's different way of thinking, behaving, and liking.

- Variety, as it is commonly known, is the spice of life – so why sweat over it – why not enjoy it. Create togetherness out of diversity.

10
RIGHTEOUSNESS

"It doesn't matter who I know or who knows me;
What matters is: do I know my self."

In the previous chapter, I introduced two behavioral-personality factors – "Variety" and "Righteousness" – that profoundly influence our behavior during relationship interactions. I annotated them as God's gift to humanity, and because I was going to make a recurring reference to these throughout my discussions, I abbreviated them as GG1 (God's Gift # 1: Variety), and GG2 (God's Gift # 2: Righteousness). You may have laughed at the hilarious mode in which I presented the "variety" factor – and, again I am going to repeat the amusing format for the "Righteousness" factor also. As before, I shall continue making a connection between GG1 (Variety) and GG2 (Arrogance) because they really are inseparable from each other.

God's Gift # 2 (GG2): Righteousness – Arrogance

"God gave us an ego, and told us that we: "know all" – "we are always right".

It seems as if, at the time of our birth, God revealed a secret in our ears. He said: "You are the only one who knows what is right – what you think and what you know is the ultimate right – the ultimate truth – the ultimate best – you know everything – and nobody knows more or better than you".

Incidentally, of course – "God said the same thing to each one of us."

The GG2: Righteousness-Arrogance syndrome can be rephrased as follows – I call it the "Omni-supreme" syndrome:
- Omni-scient: I know all
- Omni-smart: I am the smartest

- Omni-right: I am always right
- Omni-centric: All must follow me

So, these are my two ludicrous conjectures: GG1 (Variety), elaborated in the previous chapter and GG2 (Righteousness). Now you can laugh at them if you want to – but I can tell you that:

- They are a blatant reality of our being and behaving
- They exert enormous influence on our behavior
- They are a befitting analogy to our relationship scenarios.

Incidentally, I know I have annotated them as gifts of God, but every so often, I do question my judgment and ask myself whether they are really gifts of God or rather curses on humanity. Because these acts of non-acceptance of other's points of view and of being arrogant with others are really the major causes of relationship disharmony and breakings. They are the biggest instigators and creators of relationship discord, and very few of us know how to use them wisely or how to use them as gifts from God. Whether they are God's gifts or acquired entities, they can be or they have to be de-acquired or amended in order to have any hope of maintaining relationship happiness.

Elaborating GG2

GG2: Righteousness - Arrogance

- I am always right
- I know all
- What I know is the ultimate right

Personally, I think that this dimension of our personality make-up is, perhaps, the most significant of all other personality traits in terms of its derogatory impact upon our relationships. This type of behavior – of arrogance – of thinking that we are always right, even when we are not, is so prevalent and so transparent in our day-to-day relationships, that we can all notice it all around us. Yet despite its transparency, people who are seriously inflicted with this disease are very cautious in making sure that they don't portray their arrogance openly. They would utilize their righteousness stance very subtly and discreetly, without alarming you or divulging their sinister modus operandi. Just imagine how aggravating and annoying it can become when this kind of behavior is repeated endlessly in all relationship scenarios.

It is almost incomprehensible to see how we can uphold our "arrogance" stance with others, when we know that others can also do the same with us. How can relationships ameliorate amid two negatives? How can anyone tolerate continuous arrogance and still wish to maintain a happy relationship with you? If you have any desire to achieve relationship togetherness, you shall have to understand that you are not the only one who is always right, others are right too. You have to learn to show equal respect for the other's opinion also.

Actually, my observations and research indicate that this type of arrogant behavior generally emanates from people who are not very intellectual by nature or by training, and who seriously lack self-confidence in life. The result: they compensate this lack of self-confidence by being aggressive, by being prideful and arrogant, and by manifesting a behavior that announces that they know everything, even when what they know may not necessarily be right. And most likely, they do this merely to pacify or enhance their ego's false self-pride.

Not only does such behavior spoil your relationship harmony, it also deprives you of the learning process. For, when you start thinking that you know all, you stop the learning process. Then your bigotry, complacency, and arrogance takes control of your better judgment, and you automatically get sucked into the morbid cycle of low intellectuality – high pride – and low internal self-confidence. Your outside persona may be able to hide this profile of low self-confidence, but your inside persona is well aware of your shortcomings. This righteousness syndrome has, of course, a very close association with your ego, and since ego is, by itself, a very devastatingly destructive force – their collective impact makes it an even deadlier force.

Funnily – there is another anomaly in this scenario. Although it is more or less a common understanding that we are all inflicted with this disease of GG2 syndrome, none of us would ever accept this fact that we think we are always right. On the other hand, of course, each one of us would be instantly ready and prepared to say that the "other" thinks it so, but not us. We can easily vouch for and blame the other, but not our selves. To exemplify how it works, let me consider the scenario of you and your wife. Let me ask you the following:

- Do you think your spouse always thinks that he is right, and he knows everything? Most likely, you would say – yes.
- What would your spouse say if I asked him the same question about you? Most likely, he would say – yes.
- Now, I would ask you to ask this question to your own self – do you think you are always right, and that you know everything? And this is where the problem comes into play: You are either not going to accept that you do that, or you even don't know if you behave like this or not.

Now, I can make a generalization and tell you that most of us fall into this last category, where we would either not accept that we are inflicted with the disease of Omni-supreme syndrome, or we don't honestly know whether we have it or not. It's a syndrome all of us intuitively know that we have – we can feel it all around us – and we live into it and face it in our everyday relationship interactions. The problem is that since we are outward-directed energies, that is, we can observe others, but not our own self – we always feel that others have this syndrome, but we don't – not realizing, of course, that others think the same way about us. For example, Robert is ready, at a moment's notice, to give me advice on a certain issue and tell me what's right and what's not, but if, after a lapse of time, I give to him the same advice that he gave to me, on the same issue, he would probably not accept it, or possibly consider it wrong.

To further elucidate how this righteousness-arrogance syndrome can cloud our better judgment, let me take the scenario of my friend David – and this scenario is also a commonly occurring behavioral oddity with most of us. If you would have actually met David, you would have appreciated more what I am saying, but I am sure that you must have encountered similar behavioral oddities among your own friends and relatives. David is in the habit of making lofty tales and unintelligent statements, and then he would also insist that he is right. Even when ten people around David would vouch for the fact that David's claim is totally absurd and preposterous, David will keep insisting that he is right. Not only that, instead of accepting his fault, David would even put forth ten more stupid statements to defend his first stupid statement. And ultimately, if at all he does admit that he is wrong, it would only be a temporary withdrawal just to avoid the possibility of being permanently dubbed as a stupid person. Given a short passage of time, David would come back to make the same silly statement again, or another similar stupid statement – and still vehemently defend it, or defend his "Omni-supreme" syndrome. Why do we do that – why do we make a fool of our own self – why do we find it so hard to accept our fault –is it simply because of our arrogant ego?

Now, if you can project these dimensions of GG1 (Variety) and GG2 (Righteousness) onto your day-to-day relationships, you can well imagine the constant damage they can inflict on your relationship harmony. These constant argumentations, naggings, bickerings accumulate a built-up affect (the "mental-tape" effect – discussed earlier), which ultimately either destroys the relationship or puts the relationship into silent separations.

How can we understand the vagaries of GG1 (Variety) and GG2 (Righteousness)? This would only come through introspective thinking – through self-realization – through inner wisdom – to know how you behave – and then examine how it affects your relationships. A simple solution to ameliorating this process is to come to terms with your own thoughts – that you are not the only one who is right – that you are not the only one who knows all – just because God told you so. That others are can be right too – that others might know more and better than you – that God told the others also that they know all – just as much as He told you. What you need to do is:

- To understand that everyone is different – behaves and acts differently – and has a right to do so.
- To realize that everyone is as smart and as intelligent as you are.
- To appreciate and respect each other's distinct identity and point of view.
- To make an effort to create togetherness and oneness out of diversity.

Further guidelines and solutions to this issue shall be presented in section 5.

11
EGO

"Arrogance is a by-product of low self-confidence."

The Enemy Within...
- I am always ready to listen; they are not.
- I am flexible; they don't want to change.
- I know I am right.
- Why should I bend backwards?
- Why should I be the one who has to always give in?
- Hell with them – I hate them.
- I will never forgive them – never ever – until I die – even after death I will come back to haunt them.

What is that thing inside us – so prideful – so arrogant – so hateful – so vengeful – that stands in between our relationship interplay and destroys our relationships? Is it our mind – our psyche – our soul – the I – or the ego?

Whatever it is – you have to accept this fact: that there is definitely something inside us – that force – that arrogance – that pride – that person – the I – the me – which drives us, controls us, dictates our actions and behavior, and has a profound impact on our lives and relationships. And for lack of better understanding or appropriate vocabulary, I would call it what everybody else calls it – the "ego".

Our next task, therefore, is to find out:
- What is Ego?
- How does Ego influence and control our behavior?
- How can we channel the Ego-energy to our advantage?

What Is Ego

What is "Ego"? Nobody really knows what it is; all we can do is to make intelligent guesses. Ego is the most elusive entity of human being and having. But one thing is quite certain – that even when ego is very unspecific, it is still something that is somewhere there in our body – it's just that we don't know what it is and where it is. I contemplated over this question for a very long time, and the best I could come up with was that "ego" has a very close affinity with the "I", because "I" is the mainframe of our conceptualization – "I" is "me", the "person" whom we are talking about.

As such, therefore, to find out what ego is, so that I can proceed with my discussion of ego in the context of relationships, I shall present my new paradigm of the correlation of ego and the I, and then ultimately elaborate on the functioning of the ego. But before I do that, and for whatever it's worth, I would like to examine, at least for the sake of intellectual curiosity, the interrelationship of ego with other similar entities, such as the brain, mind, heart, soul, feelings, psyche, emotions, and the I. I must, however, forewarn you that my thoughts and concepts regarding the inter-relational aspects of these entities are more or less a figment of my own commonsense experiential understanding – it has no scientific basis. Typically, it has to be like that, because the nature of ego is like that also – very abstract and vague. My discussion is not going to reveal any answers, though I can guarantee you that it will definitely generate more questions. Here, then, is my dialogue:

- What is "I"?
- Is "I" the soul?
- Yes, in some ways the soul can be equated to the I when a person is dead. In a dead body, the soul is gone out and there is nobody – no "I" left inside the body – to say "I". This argument gives the impression that the I and the soul are one and the same thing.
- On the other hand – no, the I cannot be equated to the soul when we are alive. Consider, for example, when we say that my soul is hurting. This means that I am OK – the I is OK – but the soul is not – the soul is hurting – which indicates that the I and the soul are two distinguishably different entities.
- Speaking of the soul in this way, we are also, of course, making another assumption – that the soul exists – and that it runs the body motor. But, we don't even know where soul resides in the body, if at all there is something called soul.

- And, if for a moment we accept that soul exists, then it seems like that soul resides in the Heart, because when the Heart is dead, the person is dead, and the soul goes out.

- That raises another enigma – one between the Heart and the Brain – who is more powerful. Once again, it seems that the Heart is more important, because if the Brain is dead, but the Heart is functioning, the person is Brain-dead, but still alive – though not the other way around.

- Speaking of the Brain – what about the Brain and the Mind – are they the same or different entities? In an earlier chapter, I equated them to be the same just for the sake of convenience, just to make a specific point. But now I am in doubt. I think they are different. Mind is the faculty that thinks and reasons, and it does that via the machine, that is the Brain.

- I would say that the Brain and the Mind are two different entities. For, when I say: my Mind is somewhere else – that means it's not in my body – but at the same time my Brain is still physically in my body, it can't go anywhere anyway – which means that they are two different entities.

- Another interesting scenario about Brain and Mind: whenever I go to my physiotherapist, she uses ultrasound waves to relieve my pain. One time I asked her: what is the function of this therapy, and she said: the sound wave sends a message to the Brain – or befools the Brain to release natural healing chemicals, that ultimately alleviates the pain. It's a silly little example, but let's analyze it. It means that my Mind knows that my Brain is being fooled into releasing the chemicals. Clearly then, the Mind is not the same thing as the Brain – they are two different entities.

- More bizarre – if I now interject the I here – then it shows that my Mind and the I are the same, because both know that my Brain is being tricked.

- Even more bizarre – if I turn around and say that: I know that my Mind knows that the Brain is being tricked, then once again the I and the Mind become two different entities – or now we have three different entities: the I, the Mind, and the Brain.

- The same argument continues about the I being a different entity than any other part of the body, because when we say my Heart is aching, or my ears are hurting, or my legs are sore, and so on – we are connoting a separate identity for each of the body parts, as distinct from the I.

- Have we concluded that the I has a separate and unique identity and existence – if we have, then let me throw you off-balance again. What about when a person is in a coma – the Brain is temporarily dead or shut off, but the person is alive. Where is the I or the Mind gone – that something in us that cannot now, for the moment, say: hey! I am still here – it's only my Brain that is dead. It can't even say: that I am in a coma. Does that mean that the Brain, the Mind, and the I are the same? Not really, because the moment the person comes out of the coma, the I comes back, and as before, separates itself from the Mind and the Brain.

- Incidentally, where was the soul all this time when the person was in a coma?

- What about the sleep and dreams? All body parts are basically functioning in the sleep state. Even the I is alive and well, and is also taking an active part in the dreams – yet somehow, the I is not aware of the I. However, upon waking-up, the I is back again, and the I even knows and remembers the dreams in which the I was participating.

- Does that mean "I" is "awareness"? Does that mean Mind is "awareness"? Then what is awareness and where is it? Does the mind create the I or the I create the Mind? Is it that the Mind thinks of the I, and I comes into existence or the I is independent of the Mind.

Interesting, isn't it – but I am sure that even if I continue with this discussion endlessly, I would still have no answers. And by the way, I haven't even brought in the role and function of the "ego" in this whole discussion yet. Despite the fact that we have not arrived at any concrete conclusions, there is one fact that clearly emerges out of this discussion, and that is that there is an "I" that dictates our life, irrespective of whether that I is the psyche, the soul, the mind, or any other part of the body. And that is precisely the answer I was looking for. Consequently, I can now begin my new discussion to be a bit more focused on the "ego" as the integral part of the "I".

The "I" and the "Ego"

Let me now pick up the pieces, and go from one unanswerable question – "what is I" – to another unanswerable question – "what is ego" – and look at the relationship they have.

In this section, I shall present my own unproven or unprovenable (if there is any such word in the dictionary) theory about the relationship between the I and the ego, and the role ego plays in our behaviour. The only consolation I can give you this time is that, for this discussion, I am not going to lead you to more questions, but instead I am going to present a specific answer, a specific theory. This is because I have to come to a concrete conclusion about the I and the ego in order to utilize this conceptual framework of the ego for my further discussion about relationship issues. Incidentally, it should be noted that the rest of the discussion about ego in this chapter, would pertain more to the bad and damaging role that ego plays, and how it works against us to destroy our relationships, as if it is our worst enemy.

So here is my new theory. Insofar as my personal understanding goes, I think that ego is a part of the I – see the schematic. Typically, I think that the I have two components:

1. The identity part of I.
2. The self-esteem part of I.

The identity part is a simple identification and awareness of the self, such as: I am writing; I am talking; I am eating, etc. The self-esteem part is the "ego", whose function is to safeguard our self-esteem.

In the context of relationships, it is really the self-esteem part that interests me most, and therefore from here onwards, I shall consider the I and the Ego as synonyms. This would also be in line with our current concept about the ego, because we normally personify ego as "us"– the "I", for you would notice that when we speak of the ego doing this or that, we mean "us" doing this or that.

The Ego

Now that I have outlined my new perspective of the relationship of the I and the ego, I can safely digress and discuss only the "ego" part of the "I". The basic function of the ego, as far as my understanding tells me (see the diagram), is to safeguard and uphold our "self-esteem". The question is: what is self-esteem or what does ego do to safeguard it? I would answer those questions shortly, but first let me complete the discussion of my model in the schemata.

The function of safeguarding of the self-esteem can be compartmentalized into two segments:

1. Intrinsic safeguard
2. Extrinsic safeguard

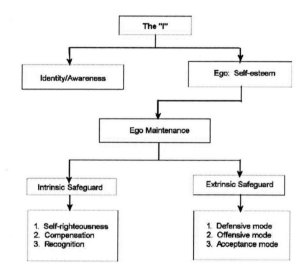

Figure 4 - Basic Functions of the Ego

The Personification of Ego

The intrinsic safeguard is related to aspects inwardly directed to the self. For example, when we self-brag about our superiority, our ego will jump in to defend our stance. This is normally done by projecting onto others our image and persona of superiority, and it is typically done via the following acts:

1. Self-righteousness
2. Compensation
3. Recognition

The extrinsic safeguard, on the other hand, is related to the reactive mode – it's our reaction to what others say to us and about us, and once again our ego stands up to fight for us. There are three reactive modes that come into play:

1. Defensive mode
2. Offensive mode
3. Acceptance mode

How Does the Ego Function

Since the role of ego is to uphold and safeguard our self-esteem, the first thing we have to know is "what is self-esteem". In the most simplistic terms, our self-esteem means – "what we think we are" – or "what our ego thinks of itself". Generally, on the mental plain, our ego thinks or wants to think very highly of itself. This is clearly evident from the way we brag about ourselves – about the things we can do, even when we don't have the capability to do what we brag about. So you can see that the role of our ego is to safeguard our "idiosyncrasies", rather than highlight our "honest-self". It is easy to realize, therefore, that our ego in not our best friend – rather on the contrary – it is our worst enemy and this enemy, unfortunately, is not out there that we can see or fight, it is inside us, and weirder – we seem to like it.

It is typically because of this negative function of our ego that we are dubbed as an "egotistic" person. And that normally is associated with a person who is low on the intellectual intelligence and honesty – is high on aggressiveness – is low on maturity – is high on arrogance – is highly stubborn – and lacks internal self-confidence. You cannot, of course, judge from this person's persona that he has low inner confidence because he displays a misleading high-energy persona. And you think he has a very high confidence level, when in fact his high-level persona is simply a compensation for his low level of internal self-esteem and self-confidence. Let us now examine how these personality traits come into play, and how our ego (or us) upholds and defends our self-presumed convictions of superiority – the righteousness stance – intrinsically and extrinsically.

Intrinsic safeguards

This relates to how we make assumptions about our superiority, and how we (or our ego) vindicate our false pretence. The discussion that I am putting forth now would also help you to understand how our behavior of, for example – arrogance, aggressiveness, immaturity, and stubbornness – involved in this process of upholding our superiority stance, can become instrumental in damaging our relationships. In the discussion above, we included three components in this category: Self-Righteousness; Compensation; and Recognition – so, let's now examine those issues.

Self-Righteousness Syndrome: This is the disease of "Omni-Supreme" syndrome that we examined in chapter 10. It relates to our conviction that we know all – we are always right – we are the smartest of all. Indeed we do it only intrinsically. For, if somebody asks us, extrinsically, if that is what we think of ourselves, we shall categorically deny it. This type of intrinsic thinking causes enormous relationship problems, because our ego (or us) keeps holding this stance stubbornly. This is, perhaps, the worst-case scenario where you can clearly see how ego controls and influences our behavior, and hence our relationship interplay and happiness. If we keep upholding this stance that we are always right – how can the other person keep tolerating it, and what if the other person also keeps behaving like that – how can the relationship even function as such?

Compensation Syndrome: A slightly milder and less harmful form of self-righteousness, the compensation mode consists of various forms of self-bragging. And they are all geared to uphold the sense of superiority and self-esteem of our ego – the superiority that we don't actually possess – a false sense of ego-pride. Bragging brings in a sense of mistrust, and the person who brags also loses his credibility and self-respect, thereby damaging himself as well as an otherwise good relationship.

Recognition Syndrome: Recognition and accolade for what we do or for our achievements is an integral part of our being, and we all vie for it. Our ego is always looking for accolade to elevate its false pride. But when the desire to achieve recognition is based on false pretense or wrong information, it destroys that sense of trust in the relationship.

Extrinsic Safeguards

These relate to the various ways in which our ego (we) fights back to defend our self-esteem when extrinsic forces attack our integrity, irrespective of whether the basis of our self-esteem claim is false or true.

Defensive Mode: In this mode, which is a milder facet of our ego, when somebody challenges our self-esteem, our reaction is generally polite and we would either stay quiet or our ego will defend our self-esteem politely.

Offensive Mode: A strong reactive mode – in this mode, if somebody challenges our integrity, we will vehemently fight back and can be obnoxiously offensive.

Acceptance Mode: If the criticism about us is positive, we may gladly accept it and try to mend our ways. If, on the other hand, the criticism is negative, we still may accept it, but we can horde anger and antagonism inside us for the other person.

Channelling the Ego-Energy

We humans! We really are nothing but – walking – talking – arrogant – taut egos. We are feelings and emotions machines. We really don't know what ego is, or where it resides in our body, and how elusive an entity it is – yet we know that it is almost the most powerful force that controls and influences our personality, behavior, and relationships. As long as our ego controls us, and we are slaves to it, our relationships would never get a fair chance to ameliorate.

We all have egos – yet:

- Many of us don't either know we are egotists or won't admit.
- Many of us would refuse to accept that our ego is a serious impediment in the way of our relationship harmony.
- None of us will ever accept that ego controls us. Instead, we would all jump up to say that we are in full control of our life.

These facets of ego are clearly evidenced through the manifestation of your daily, routine attitude and behavior, such as: you behave arrogantly with each other, but won't admit that you do – you behave aggressively with each other, but won't accept that you do – in almost every situation, you think you are right, not the other – you are always ready to give advice, but never accept it. The problem is that if each one of us stays in that hyped-up egotistic state of mind, then how can life function – how can we ever hope to strike a compromise – how can we ever create permanent relationship harmony or even hope to just barely maintain a relationship.

Fortunately, after considerable contemplation, I came to the conclusion that there is, indeed, a solution to the problem – that there is a way we can re-channel this ego-energy to our advantage. Basically, the solution involves the following three actions:

- Drop the ego
- Develop mindfulness
- Humble the ego

Drop the Ego

I shall discuss the first two items: drop the ego and mindfulness, together in this section. To begin with, I would like to take you back, for a moment, to the basic questions again: what is this phantom that we call the ego; and how do we create this phantom?

Let's first try to qualify what ego is. Ego is a hypothetical phantom created by our mental imagery. Whenever we are challenged, threatened, insulted, mistreated, or emotionally hurt, by any which means, we wake up our phantom to fight for us – to fight back to safeguard our identity and self-esteem. This phantom is not created each time or incidence-by-incidence, it is created permanently, once and for all, and stored somewhere inside us – but it is always ready and armed to fight back at a moment's notice.

Unfortunately, the story doesn't end there. The phantom does not only wake up when there is an actual external stimulus or intervention. We can also wake him up by creating a hypothetical fight through our mental imagery and keep our ego-phantom hyped-up in a fight, which was never there in reality. Just by thinking and ruminating about things and incidences, we can, through the inside built-up anger and antagonism, wake up the phantom through hypothetical imagery and start fighting the hypothetical fight. And since we humans are so highly feelings-sensitive, a puff of wind, much less an angry statement, can tilt our emotional balance and our phantom comes to life to fight for us.

Now, let me go into the concept of "dropping the ego". It's a very beautiful concept on "how to control your ego" – and I shall again re-discuss it in chapter 25. Ego has two modes – a waking mode, and a sleeping mode. Most of the time, the ego is in the waking mode, but there are moments of time, when it is sleeping – not interfering with your behavior and actions. And these are the moments that I annotate as the "dropped ego" moments. Let me explain it by taking a few scenarios of these moments.

Consider the scenario when you are relaxing on a beach. You are totally relaxed, calm, happy, and fulfilled. Do you know why – because your ego is sleeping, there is no ego for the moment – no association with the memories – no upholding of pride or self-esteem – the "ego is dropped". Suddenly however, in the split of a second, your state of calmness can change into anguish, if you start thinking of some bad incidence from your memory bank. Why does that happen? It is because your ego is back again – you are tense again, even when you are still on the beach – and the beach and the waters are still the same – calm and serene. Only now, you are not relaxed, you are tense because your ego is awake. So you see how ego can be dropped by disassociation or brought back to life via association with the mind – the memories – the accumulation.

Here are some other situations where the ego is dropped: when you listen to music; when you are making love; when you are eating your favourite food – in all these situations, you are at peace with yourself because, for that moment, you are single-focused – the ego is sleeping and not interfering with your behavior.

Ego is also dropped when you are silent or when you are meditating because there is no "center" – no "crystallized I". In silence, you can enter the ego-less domain – then the mind will see reality as reality. This is what is known as the state of "mindfulness".

When this idea came to me, I suddenly felt that I have the answer to how to control the ego. For I said to myself that if there are moments when the ego is sleeping – the ego is dropped – that means the ego is droppable – and as such, it is controllable. Which means that if we can learn how to mimic and artificially induce such moments and learn how to generate and elongate those moments of time when the ego is silent and sleeping, we can tame the ego. What are the characteristics of those moments when the ego is sleeping – they are the moments when you are staying in the present, rather than jumping into the past, the memories – or jumping into the future, the domain of "non-reality".

This is where I want to introduce a new thought, the thought that I annotate as "freeze-frame" the moments – staying in the present. Whenever you stay in the present, you are focused exclusively on the task at hand – the ego is dropped because ego is only either the past or the future. So if you can learn how to freeze-frame those moments more often and for longer periods of time, you can control the ego, and you can achieve a state of "mindfulness" – a state of peacefulness in relationships. And if you can learn how to generate such moments at will – moments when the ego is absent, you can master the art of ego-control. Such moments will get you in the habit of going inside your consciousness, and help provide you with the strength to permanently block your ego from interfering with your relationships, resulting in sustainable relationship harmony.

Humble the Ego

Ego is problematic, simply because it is too taut, too stubborn, and highly uncompromising. How do we humble the ego? Humbling down the whole ego all at once is next to impossible. But there is a simple recipe you can try to make the impossible possible – it involves two things: working on an incident-by-incident or moment-by-moment basis to mellow the ego; and working in such a way that the ego doesn't get alarmed and conscious of the fact that you are trying to humble him down.

What does "humbling down" your ego, mean? It means bending backwards to be more compromising, to be saying "yes's" more often than "no's" in your relationship interactions – to become more positive and humble.

As an example, suppose that your spouse is saying something to you that you know is not right, but still he wants you to agree with him that he is right. If you keep agreeing and saying, "yes" to all such situations, you probably feel you are being stupid. But, on the other hand, think of the other scenario – that if you keep saying "no", the fight would never end. So why don't you just try saying "yes" – at least just once – even when you know he is wrong? You would be amazed that the impact of one "yes" may be far greater than a thousand "no's". And the fight will stop. After a while, your spouse may also humble down and realize that what he was saying or insisting upon was not right – he may feel ashamed of his own behavior, and then you will be able to connect with him more easily to ameliorate the situation.

So, what is the end result – you win the game just by humbling down your own ego for that moment of time – and the purpose was to win anyway – and in the process – you humbled the other person's ego as well. So if you can get into the habit of humbling down your ego — incidence by incidence — moment by moment — you may end up winning every time.

This now concludes our discussion of the "ego" — the most important and the most elusive of the personality traits that affects our thinking, behavior, and relationship togetherness. In chapter 25, we shall once again open up our discussion to find out how to control and channel the ego.

12
AGGRESSIVENESS

"The greatest disgrace comes
when you have fallen in your own eyes."

Next to ego, the characteristic of Aggressiveness of our personality plays the most dominant role in life and relationships. While ego is a sort of elusive entity, aggressiveness we can clearly actualize and appreciate. While ego, for the most part, may be considered a curse to humanity, aggressiveness can be the greatest gift or the worst curse, depending on how you control it and utilize it.

Aggressiveness is paramount to human achievement and success, at least in the more materialistic sense. Right amount of aggressiveness, combined with high levels of maturity, knowledge, and wisdom, can make a person a source of inspiration and leadership for everyone. However, when aggressiveness goes beyond the threshold of assertiveness, it becomes obnoxious and egotistic. In this mode, it negatively affects a person's maturity and intelligence and consequently becomes a source of relationship breakdowns.

With this premise, I shall now examine the following aspects of aggressiveness:

- The nature and characteristic of aggressiveness.
- Aggressiveness and the sex differences.
- The impact of aggressiveness on relationships.
- Controlling and channelling aggressiveness.

What is Aggressiveness

Like the sixth sense, aggressiveness is that extra gusto and drive that we have – the force – the energy – the vigour – the dynamism – that pushes us to achieve the unachievable. The distribution of this energy is manifested in varying degrees in different people, and as well, its characteristics are also differently exhibited by different people.

There are, basically, two facets of aggressiveness: positive and negative.

- Positive Mode: drive, dynamism, zeal, assertiveness, passion, determination – that forceful and obtrusive energy and drive for the pursuit of one's goals.
- Negative Mode: pushy, hostile, egotistic, arrogant, obnoxious, dominating – a disposition to dominate, often in disregard of the other person's feelings.

In this book, our main preoccupation is towards the negative aspects of aggressiveness because those are the ones that bear a strong impact on our relationships.

Characteristics of Aggressiveness

What are the characteristics of an aggressive person?

People are good judges of people. To a greater or lesser degree, we all have the ability – that sixth sense – to size up people. As you can notice, you often hear people saying, "John is very aggressive". And it is also not too difficult to infer whether they are speaking about John's positive or negative aggressiveness, because the tone and context of their observation will indicate the nature of the aggressiveness.

How do you judge whether a person is aggressive or not? I guess this is a matter of a keen sense of observation. I have my own rudimentary built-in gauge by which I assess a person's aggressiveness, and I can share it with you. There are two aspects of a person that would give me an indication of a person's aggressiveness: physical appearance, and behavior.

In terms of the physical appearance, it is generally the eyes and the area around the eyes that would manifest the signs of aggressiveness. The eyes are a window to a person's personality. Examine the eyes first – aggressive eyes are generally:

- Small – sort of closed – not too big or open
- Sharp, searching, shrewd looking
- As if full of anger
- Focused and attentive – consciously aware

Now examine the area around the eyes – it is generally:

- Taut – not soft or pleasant
- Marked by a stressful look
- Anger-filled, fierce and dominating looking

These are some of the general observational characteristics, and they vary from person to person. Also, it should be noted that this scenario is more befitting to men than women because both sexes have different appearance characteristics of aggressiveness. Women's facial appearance, in the context of aggressiveness, is slightly different, though they would also have many of those characteristics of aggressiveness as men have. Women's aggressiveness is manifested more via their behavior and actions.

Besides the eyes, of course, there are many other indicators of the person's behavior that shed light on how aggressive the person is – noting, of course, that there are always person-to-person differences in the level or degree of aggressiveness. Let us look at some of those behavioral characteristics that separate an aggressive person from the rest of the crowd. An aggressive person:

- Is pushy
- Wants to dominate the scene by talking and telling others what is right or wrong – strongly giving his opinion, and forcefully indicating that what he is saying and thinking is right – the only ultimate right – and he would do this very subtly, so that he doesn't give anyone the impression that he is being pushy.
- Is a poor listener? In fact, even when he is listening, he is not attentive because he is simply thinking of what he is going to say when the other person has finished speaking – or even worse – he would abruptly interrupt the other person, in order to say what he wants to say.
- Constantly manifests restlessness via his bodily gestures
- Is always in a state of hurriedness.
- Manifests immature, unbalanced, and egotistic behavior
- Is always running around in life in search of solace and happiness, because he is usually very unhappy and unfulfilled inside.

Nature and Types of Aggressiveness

Typically, we all possess aggressiveness traits in varying degrees, and its manifestation is also different in different individuals. In the behavioral arenas, aggressiveness doesn't operate independently or in isolation, it is generally accompanied by and influenced by other characteristics such as emotions, immaturity, and ego. Highly aggressive people are generally highly egotistic also, and when their behavior is dictated by their emotions, rather than by their intellect, the first calamity is their maturity. Aggressiveness directly impacts maturity — most aggressive people tend to be rather immature in their interplay of relationships.

Within the framework of "high aggressiveness", I will now outline the salient characteristics of some of the different types of aggressiveness:

1. **Positive Aggressiveness**: the best and greatest gift one can have — for instance, a combination of right amounts of positive aggressiveness, maturity, and wisdom can make the person a leader and a great companion to have a relationship with. And the good news is that this trait is achievable through personal endeavour.

2. **Negative Aggressiveness**: the opposite end of the positive spectrum — where the person is pushy, unapproachable, uncompromising, highly arrogant, and lacking in maturity — a perfect scenario for unhappy relationships.

3. **Mature Aggressiveness**: where the person is intelligent, subtle, mature, has a good thinking mind — and utilizes his aggressiveness to his advantage.

4. **Silent Aggressiveness**: this category includes people that are positively and maturely aggressive, but more quietly and subtly. They don't wish to dominate the scene — they talk less and listen more — but when they talk, and they do talk only when they make good sense, they like to be listened to as attentively as they listened to others when others were speaking. They are consciously aware of their aggressiveness, but they don't try to push or dominate — and in the same token, they don't like to be pushed either. This group is very sensitive to relationships, and they believe in mutual respect and companionship.

5. **Persona Aggressiveness**: these people are neither truly nor intellectually aggressive, but they show off and manifest a persona that indicates that they are aggressive, and that is generally to gain some kind of advantage.

6. **Talkative Aggressiveness**: this group gives the impression, by their incessant yap-yap, that they are aggressive and dominating, but in reality they are not very aggressive.

Irrespective of the aggressiveness types, there are a few universal facts that should be noted:

- Many people don't even know that they are aggressive.
- Most aggressive people would never directly admit that they are pushy, aggressive, and dominating, even when they are.
- Of the people who would admit that they are aggressive, they do so because of one or more of the following reasons:
   They are honest.
   They want to show off their arrogance – a way to satisfy and elevate their ego's false pride.
   They associate aggressiveness with power, authority, and elegance.
   They want to make some kind of gains by showing off that they are aggressive.

Aggressiveness: Men versus Women

Men and women are different in every respect – genetic as well as behavioral – and that's an indisputable fact. They are also different with respect to the level, intensity, and manifestation of aggressiveness. As such, therefore, it is important to understand those differences, because those differences influence our behavior and attitude, and they are the main source of problems arising in marital relationships.

I made a statement earlier that men are more aggressive than women. Before we go any further, I must clarify my stance:

- I am only speaking in terms of generalities, just to generate a dialogue – for we all know that some women can be even more aggressive than men.
- Also, in discussing aggressiveness, we are not labelling anything as good or bad – right or wrong – superior or inferior. Aggressiveness is just a trait – you either have it or you don't. What we want to understand is how to control and utilize it effectively and manage it wisely.

Women – even when they are seemingly less aggressive than men – are generally more aggressively in control of their home front in all phases of life, irrespective of whether they work or stay home, and irrespective of whether men are more aggressive in the Breakfast and Lunch phases. Women manifest less aggressiveness in the Breakfast and Lunch phases because these are the phases of making the relationship, not breaking – and also because women are makers and givers of life, rather than takers. Somehow though, either by virtue of what has transpired in the first two phases of relationships and life or otherwise, women tend to assume greater aggressiveness in the Dinner phase, as if they pick up from where the men left off.

Men are generally more aggressive in the Breakfast and Lunch phases of life. In the Dinner phase, they become more mellow and subtle. Men's aggressiveness is generally associated with work and achievement. It is generally not mixed up with the home front, where women are in total and absolute control, irrespective. However, some men do tend to exert their aggressiveness of work and success at the home front also, which is what becomes the main source of relationship problems.

Let's examine these sex differences relating to aggressiveness in the context of a marital relationship and see how they impact the relationship game. We shall examine the following four different combinations:

- Women more aggressive than men.
- Men more aggressive than women.
- Both partners highly aggressive
- Both partners not aggressive.

1. **Women More Aggressive Than Men**

At the courtship time, both men and women are equally careful to make sure that they don't go out of their way to exhibit their aggressiveness, because at that time, there is an inherent desire and necessity to consummate the relationship. After the marriage, if the woman is more aggressive, then she will quickly assume control and responsibility of, at least, the home and social matters. If the man is not very aggressive and he accepts his and her level of aggressiveness, then this marriage should last forever. The only way in which this scenario can run into problems is if the woman becomes unbearably pushy, or the man also becomes aggressive and intolerant of the woman's aggressiveness.

So, within the confines of their own closed loop of life and relationship, this combination – of woman being more aggressive than man – should not run into any relationship problems, as long as both parties have accepted their respective aggressiveness roles. Problems could still arise, however, in the extended relationship domain – that of relatives and friends – because a very highly aggressive woman, for a start, would not allow or tolerate any interference by the relatives, especially from the husband's side, howsoever genuine and important that may be. It fact, she may be hostile to relatives, because she may be blinded by her self-assumption, that if she can push her husband around, then surely she can bully other relatives too, and this causes a direct hit on the relationship harmony. Again, its funny that sometimes, even these women don't themselves know that they are so aggressive and pushy – and worse – even if you tell them so, they will never ever admit that they are dominating. To some extent, highly aggressive women have less ability and maturity to control their aggressiveness as compared to their male counterparts.

There is another funny paradox about these highly aggressive-type women: on one hand, they intuitively enjoy the feeling that they control their husband, but on the other hand, they also complain that their husband is a moron – a sissy – doesn't behave like a man – like other men do – as men should behave. Funny, she forgets to realize that she is the one who has reduced him to nothing – to a sissy – in the first place – so why is she complaining now. As a matter of fact, highly aggressive women always end up making their husbands weak.

2.   Men More Aggressive Than Women

If the man is aggressive, and the woman is not, the following can ensue:

- The relationship can go on if the man can limit his aggressiveness to the work front only and not bring it home on a continuous basis, that is, if he lets the woman run the household the way she wants to, because that's her domain anyway.
- Even if the man brings his aggressiveness home, the relationship may still go on if the woman accepts it, or in some situations, where the woman has no other recourse but to accept it.
- The relationship has a high probability of going bad in the Dinner phase if the woman becomes more aggressive and the man still upholds his aggressiveness rather than becoming more mellow. In this situation, the relationship can either go into silent separations or actually break also.

3.   Both Men and Women Aggressive

When the man and the woman are both equally and seriously aggressive, we have a perfect scenario for disaster – for a life-long fight to death. Two things can happen:

- Either they will break the relationship fairly soon after marriage, or

- If they decide not to separate, but to stick to each other, and get used to each other's aggressiveness, then they will almost have an unending life of bickering and naggings, and they can be in a virtual state of silent separations all their life

I know a perfect case scenario of my friend Robert and his wife Sue. Robert and Sue are both very aggressive – from day one. They are still together – never separated – stuck with each other after 40 years of married life, yet never saw eye to eye with each other. Both are very dominating – wanting to dominate the other – wanting to let the other down. They criticize each other, even in front of others in a social gathering – stonewalling each other – never compromising – always trying to prove the other wrong. A whole life has gone into fighting and bickering. They still don't admit that their life has been one hell of a mess, though everyone else around them knows pretty well that their married life has been a total failure. Robert and Sue are a perfect scenario for "silent separations" – "lonesome-togetherness". If you recall, this is the example I quoted at the beginning of the book – Robert saying to me:

**"I was lonely, so I got married;
Now, we are two lonely people."**

**"At night when we sleep together in our beds;
It feels like as if two graves are lying side-by-side."**

**"Now they don't even sleep together in the same room – they
sleep in different rooms – one grave per room."**

The only brighter side to their marriage – and the reason why they have not separated until now – is because they have accepted each other's aggressiveness. They don't interfere with each other's affairs, and the marriage goes on – two individual marriages – his and hers – not one.

I must identify another scenario here, which may seem contradictory to the ones I have listed above, yet it is within the frame of reference when both the man and the woman are aggressive. If, while being very aggressive, they are also both very mature and intelligent, and they complement each other's strengths and weaknesses rather than interfering or criticizing each other, then they can make a great team and a great marriage.

4. Both Men and Women Not Aggressive

This is a situation in which the likelihood of the relationship going bad is almost minimal or at least because of aggressiveness. Of course, the relationship can go bad because of many other factors.

The above discussion provides a strong indication that marital relationships always hang loose in the delicate balance of aggressive attitudes of the spouses. Aggressiveness is, undoubtedly, the single most dominant factor responsible for causing relationship breakdowns. I think if you ever dig into the statistics of reasons for separations/divorces, you find aggressiveness is the primary cause-effect. We all know that we cannot tolerate each other's aggressive attitude, yet we still keep behaving like that and as such, we keep ourselves constantly locked up in unhappy relationships. This is absolutely idiosyncratic. Finally, by whichever gauge you may measure people, a high level of negative aggressiveness is bad in every respect because

- Aggressive people are a source of irritation for everyone.
- Aggressive people hurt others, and in the process, they also get hurt.
- Aggressiveness hurts emotions – and that puts the ego on guard – and the whole chain reaction of anger and antagonistic feelings ensues.

Under no circumstances would we be able to materialize relationship togetherness and harmony unless we can break through this morbid cycle of ego-aggressiveness and work towards channelling this negative-aggressive energy to generate a mutually respectful positive behavior and attitude.

Controlling and Channelling Aggressiveness

In an attempt to bring about changes in our attitudes, we first need to find out if aggressiveness is a controllable entity, that is, does it lend itself to changes? Fortunately, yes it does – because when we look around, we find that some people can alter their behavior, while others cannot. Which means that it is possible to tame our aggressiveness and channel the negative energy to generate a positive disposition. It, of course, requires conscientious effort to do that.

We are a product of thinking, emotions, feelings, and personality characteristics. Our actions and decisions are impacted by these entities. What we need to understand is how and in what proportion these entities impact our decisions because that's what determines the quality and appropriateness of our actions? Most people with aggressive personality characteristics, who tend to be ruled and dictated by their emotions, tend to mal-utilize their abilities, and consequently end up hurting their relationships. Those people, who have the maturity and ability to properly channel their thinking, and control their aggressiveness to their advantage, end up remaining in happy relationships.

Aggressiveness can easily be channelled into positive energy by the following three-step process:

- Self-realization: to have full awareness of the fact that you have the tendency to be aggressive, and to know the extent of your aggressiveness.
- Self-acceptance: to come to terms with yourself and your ego, to accept the fact that your behavior is aggressive, and it needs to be modified.
- Desire to harness: to have a genuine and honest desire and determination to reduce or eliminate your aggressiveness in your relationship interactions.

Further guidelines on how to tame and channel your aggressiveness are appended in chapter 26.

13
MATURITY

"If you love somebody;
Then why try to change what you love."

In the previous chapter, while discussing the impact of aggressiveness on our relationship interactions, we also briefly identified how aggressiveness affects a person's maturity level. Now we shall continue from where we left off and elaborate the subject a bit further. In addition, we shall also discuss the role of some other important characteristics of personality such as knowledge, wisdom, and shrewdness, which are closely associated with maturity, and have a significant impact on our behavior. As I have asserted before, personality traits have a circular interrelationship with each other, and it is the collective impact of all traits, in different degrees, that really impacts our personality, behavior, and relationships. In that context, I wish to examine the interrelationship of maturity with aggressiveness, ego, wisdom, knowledge, and stupidity – while at the same time identifying how maturity affects our behavior.

What is Maturity

Maturity is hard to define in isolation because it doesn't pertain to a singular personality characteristic or ability – it's a dimension of several factors put together. However, in general terms, maturity can be defined as that subtle fullness and wisdom of one's personality – a combination of inner stability, humbleness, calmness, wisdom, and empathy.

How do you assess a person's maturity level? I think the best possible way is through a keen sense of observation of how a person behaves, acts – his mannerisms and gestures – his speech and actions, and other behavioral factors, such as the following:

- His calmness and relaxed state of mind
- His thoughtfulness, patience, and balanced stability
- His respect and care for other's feelings and sensitivities

- The way he asks or answers questions
- The way he presents his own point of view and opinions
- The way he attentively listens to others
- His judiciousness and fairness
- His sense of empathy and gentleness
- His unhurried gestures
- His sense of time and place to say something

These are just some of the many ways in which you can get a sense of how mature and wise a person is. A mature person is certainly very conducive to building and maintaining a healthy relationship. On the other hand, constant immature behavior – intentional or unintentional – can become a source of irritability and discomfort in any relationship. Over a long period of time, immature behavior tends to cause a build-up of anger and feelings of irritability, and this can cause a slow degeneration of the relationship, leading to silent separations.

Maturity – Aggressiveness

Maturity and aggressiveness have a very strong one-to-one inverse relationship. When aggressiveness goes up, maturity goes down – almost automatically. It is not too difficult to pick up the person with low maturity and high negative aggressiveness because his actions will manifest a hurried look, lack of stability, and an imbalanced state of mind. And if you want further confirmation of your assessment of his level of immaturity, you can notice from his speech and behavior that he has the tendency to make untenable claims and unintelligent statements. Everybody around him would know how ridiculously baseless his claims are, but he is the only one who can't see through that. Even weirder – not only would he not withdraw his statement or accept his idiosyncratic stance, he would instead put forth ten more stupid statements to defend his first stupid statement. Why is it so? Because his immaturity, aggressiveness, and ego-pride overrides his wisdom, and they won't let him accept defeat, even when defeat translates into being mature and wise.

All it needs is for him to say, at the onset, that I am sorry – that I think what I am saying is not right. By God! How difficult it is for us humans to say that? It is such a simple action, that a one-minute of humbling down, and that, too, for a right cause, can save him from being dubbed as a stupid and stubborn person. All it needs is a bit of self-awareness and self-control, and half a teaspoon full of wisdom, in order to neutralize that momentary bout of stupidity, aggressiveness, and egotism.

Why does this stupidity overpower our sound judgment – why do we behave like this when we humans are really supposed to be intelligent beings? Is this an unconscious act or a conscious behavior? Personally, I believe that there is no such thing as inherent stupidity – in the sense of unconscious foolishness or plain dumb-headedness – unless, of course, it's a medical condition. I think our stupid behavior may be due to the fact that:

- We let aggressiveness, ego, and immaturity override our actions.
- We may want to gain some kind of advantage by posing to be stupid.
- We may want to get away from being blamed for an action – by posing our innocence under the veil of stupidity – when, in reality, it is plain cunningness.

I think, a conscious-level stupid person, generally, has a combination of high aggressiveness, low maturity, high false arrogance and pride, an unhappy outlook on life, and a lot of unfulfillment. Generally, a conscious-level stupid person thinks that he is very clever and smart, that he knows all and the whole truth, that others are stupid and they won't know what he is up to. And this is because a stupid person thinks he is very shrewd, and he equates shrewdness to wisdom. Unfortunately, I equate shrewdness to cunningness, or at least, in the context of relationships.

Let me interject a funny analogy here. Let me vaguely and hypothetically personify how God, in His production plant, distributes wisdom and shrewdness to humans. I think:

- To some, He gives two parts wisdom;
- To others, He gives one part wisdom and one part shrewdness;
- And when He runs short of wisdom, because wisdom is in short supply – to some He gives two parts shrewdness, and He has plenty of that.

Now, to those whom He gives two parts shrewdness or cunningness, just to console them and pacify them so that they don't feel that God has been unfair to them, He assures them that they are the most intelligent, that they know the whole truth, that others are stupid compared to them. In my terminology, I think it is just a booster shot of "Omni-Supreme" syndrome that God gives to these people. Funny – isn't it? I know it's a naive analogy, but still, it helps me to make my point anyway.

There we are – we now have a combination of immaturity, aggressiveness, and shrewdness – and what do we get – a perfect candidate for bad relationships. These are the kinds of collective behavior patterns – of aggressiveness, immaturity, and cunningness – which imparts an image of stupidity on the person's profile, and which are instrumental for the slow, but steady, deterioration of the relationship harmony. Let me close this discussion with another funny analogy about stupidity:

- A stupid person doesn't know that he is stupid because he is stupid – for if he knew he was stupid, he wouldn't be stupid anymore.
- You can't tell a stupid person that he is stupid because he won't understand – why – because he is stupid.
- In fact, you are being stupid yourself to tell a stupid person that he is stupid – knowing well that he is stupid and won't understand what you are saying.

Maturity, Knowledge and Wisdom

Now, let's look at the other side of the scale of maturity, where knowledge and wisdom are housed, and examine their collective role and impact on our behavior. Here are some of my random thoughts on the subject:

- Knowledge is extremely important. It constitutes: general understanding and comprehension, basic education and training, and judgmental ability.
- But knowledge is not wisdom. Wisdom is far above knowledge, though knowledge helps to accentuate wisdom.
- Knowledge comes from the outside – wisdom comes from within.
- Knowledge is the product of mind – wisdom is the power of the soul.
- Wisdom is:
  o that inner fullness, maturity, and stability;
  o to know when to speak and when to listen;
  o to know how to strike a balance between thinking and action;

o   to know how to balance between being and having;

o   to know how to do the right thing – at the right time and place – in the right way – for the right reason – with the right intention – with the right awareness – and with the right people.

- Knowledge can betray you – wisdom will never let you down.
- Knowledge can lead you to arrogance and ignorance – wisdom will guide you back to sanity.

God – in His infinite wisdom – has given wisdom to everyone. A few people keep their wisdom completely locked up within themselves. They either don't know if they have it or don't know how to harness this power. Others know how to self-utilize and enhance their wisdom. They also distribute and share their wisdom benevolently with others. The awakening, the realization, and the utilization of that dormant energy inside us – the wisdom – is totally dependent on us and our desires and efforts.

Recapitulating the thoughts – we can see that there is a circular relationship operating here. A high level of negative aggressiveness affects your sense of maturity, and when maturity is down, you tend to be more aggressive. The more aggressiveness we show, the more our ego feels happy – and more immaturely we act. It is all in the act of the ego – our worst enemy, who misguides our actions. And when ego feels happy, we try to be even more aggressive, even at the cost of maturity – and weirdly enough, we even feel proud of our actions.

Along with this thought, let me now close my discussion by suggesting a few simple rules for accentuating your sense of maturity:

- Inculcate a habit of speaking slowly and thoughtfully – not abruptly, impulsively, or aggressively. Speak with confidence.
- Speak honestly, factually, truthfully, and with a positive mindset.
- Don't repeat your stories over and over again – people get tired of listening to your lofty tales.
- Develop a sense of calmness, humbleness, and patience.
- Be a good listener also – don't constantly interrupt people.
- Don't just keep talking – give others a chance to say something.

- Be judicious, respectful, and appreciate others' point of view.
- Give up arrogance and the feeling that you know all — that others are stupid — that you are always right. Know that others can be right also — and that you can be wrong also.

14
THINKING

"It is so easy to say – I am angry with you;
And, so difficult to say – I love you."

This chapter is not about the normal and natural process of thinking that we do for life and living, it is about the conscious-level internalized process of emotional thinking that sets the tone for our personality profile and establishes the framework of our behavior and attitude – it is what makes us "us". We are what we think, but also what we think is because of what we are – it's a circular relationship. Whatever personality make-up we have influences the way we think, and that would impact our relationships. Or, on the other hand, whatever and howsoever we think would have an influence in giving us a type of personality we have, and that impacts our behavior and attitude.

If we have a positive outlook on life, we will think positively and behave and act positively. And when we continuously think positively, our personality becomes permanently positive. Positive thinking generates a positive personality, and a positive personality generates positive relationships. If we have a negative disposition, we will think negatively, and our day-to-day interactions would be in the negative mode. A perpetual negative mode would make us a negative person.

Relationships do go bad because of what we say to each other – but that error-prone message is merely a by-product of our thinking and personality. Whatever we say to each other is not merely a matter of words and speech – it's a reflection of what we are and how we think – a mirror of our personality profile – the person we are.

Types of Thinkers

In this chapter, I wish to consider various types of thinkers, and various modes of thinking in order to examine how this entire thinking framework affects our behavior. Starting with the type of thinkers, although the range of thinkers is very wide, for the sake of brevity, I would divide people into the two broad categories: Type A: Outward-Directed Thinkers; and Type B: Inward-Directed Thinkers. It should be noted that the focus of my discussion is in the context of relationships only.

Type A: Outward-Directed Thinkers

These are the people with outward-directed energies – they always see the faults of others, but never their own. And this is because they are also inflicted with the serious disease of "righteousness" – the "Omni-Supreme syndrome" that I elucidated in chapter 10. These people have an unflinching conviction that they are always right – that they know everything – and that what they know is the ultimate truth – because God has told them so. They are, therefore, always ready to give advice, but never to accept advice because they know everything, and therefore, they don't need advice. We have lots of them – they are in absolute majority – they are all around us – and they are the ones who make the relationship journey so utterly torturous. What these people don't realize is that everybody else thinks the same way – and at the same time, everybody is different? So, we have a whole population of different people, all thinking that they are right and the other is wrong – and all wanting to live into relationships of togetherness, oneness, and happiness – wow! What a "royal mess".

Type B: Inward-Directed Thinkers:

These are highly sensitive and emotional people. They have as much self-esteem or ego or aggressiveness as the outward-directed ones, yet they respect the other person's self-esteem, behavior, and personality make-up as it is. The powerhouse of their energy is their inner wisdom, which comes through the process of introspective thinking, by which they activate inner-awakenings and inner-evolution. Whenever relationship problems occur, they can easily resolve the problems themselves because they are feeling-sensitive people, and they have good analytical capabilities. The only weakness of Type B is over-sensitiveness and excessive emotionality. This can make them a bit introverted at times, and it can lead to negativity. But, all in all, they are makers rather than breakers of relationships.

Modes of thinking

The various thinking modes can be broadly classified as follows:

1. Phantom Thinking
2. Extrinsic-Persona Thinking
3. Intrinsic-Persona Thinking
4. Extrinsic-Envy Thinking
5. Intrinsic-Unfulfillment Thinking
6. Setting-The-World-Right Thinking
7. Mental-Tape Thinking
8. Righteousness (GG2) Thinking
9. Misunderstanding-Misinterpretation Thinking

1. **Phantom Thinking:** This is the mode in which your mind makes up all kinds of negative imagery about people – how they would behave or act with you – even when they have not even interacted with you. You can create all sorts of negative feelings and perceptions that have no realistic basis, and as such, this mode can put you in a perpetual state of anger and antagonism about others. This is the most dangerous of all thinking modes – especially for relationships.

2. **Extrinsic-Persona Thinking:** In this mode, your overall preoccupation is about how others perceive you, what they think of you, and their feelings and impressions about you. Your self-acceptance is, in a way, connected to others' acceptance of you. This mode, though not directly dangerous, can inculcate a feeling of anger and mistrust that is directed onto others, for no reason or fault of the others, but your own – and it can become an impediment in the progression of a harmonious relationship.

3. **Intrinsic-Persona Thinking:** This mode is the reverse of the above, where you are constantly worried about your own image – as you yourself perceive it. To some extent, it's a positive entity, because it involves introspective thinking, which brings you awareness and awakening. But in the extreme case, it can generate a sense of lack of self-confidence, which can adversely affect your relationships, directly or indirectly.

4. **Extrinsic-Envy Thinking:** This mode relates to comparative and competitive aspects of life and living, more on the materialistic side: money, fame, love, health, etc. Here, your thinking and feelings are loaded with jealousy, envy, and anger, and it is directed to those people who have more than what you have. This mode will clearly hinder the smooth and compassionate flow of feelings in your relationships.

5. **Intrinsic-Unfulfillment Thinking:** Like the above extrinsic-envy mode, this one is also related to materialistic aspects, but directed to your own self by yourself. It pertains to your own fantasies and desires for materialistic things: money, fame, love, etc. – wanting to have what you don't have. Constant thinking in this mode can plague you with a perpetual sense of unfulfillment that can impoverish your self-confidence.

6. **Setting-The-World-Right Thinking:** This is the most dangerous mode of thinking, because it is an anger-filled mode. It has no designated target – it is directed to the whole world – you want to set the world right – you want to teach everyone a lesson, the hard way – you want to punish anyone who doesn't do things right – and the "right" is your right – what you think is right – not the world's right. This makes you a very aggressive, anger-filled, and negative person. It is a dangerous mode of thinking, not only for relationships, but also for all aspects of life and living.

7. **Mental-Tape Thinking:** This subject has been amply discussed earlier in Chapter 8. It is a mode in which you have a tendency to hoard negative feelings, rather than letting things go, and you carry your relationship on the basis of those pent-up feelings. This mode doesn't give the relationship a fair chance to ameliorate, and it can, therefore, cause serious relationship problems.

8. **Righteousness (GG2) Thinking:** This mode has already been elaborated in Chapter 10. This personality trait is such that it makes you think that you know everything, and that what you know is the only and ultimate right. At the same time, you think that others don't know as much as you do, or that they are less intelligent than you. Consequently, you are always

ready to criticize others on what they do, and you are always ready to offer advice. But on the other hand, you don't like to accept criticism on what you do, nor are you willing to accept advice. You uphold that uncanny conviction in your mind that others are stupid and they need advice, but not you, because you know everything. At times, you would criticize somebody for something, and within a span of a very short time, you may do the same thing yourself – but now it is not wrong, it is acceptable because now you are doing it, and you are always right anyway. The problem, as indicated earlier, is that it's not only you who feels like this – everyone else thinks the same way – which raises the obvious question – "who is right" and "how can relationships ever function under these circumstances".

9. **Misunderstanding-Misinterpretation Thinking:** This is the most commonly occurring scenario in relationships. Day-in and day-out, we all experience how we fight and bicker with each other on what the other "said" or "not said", or what you understood from what he said. Misunderstandings are the number one cause of the daily annoyances of relationship life, and their cumulative affect becomes instrumental in creating a negative mental-tape, which ultimately leads to a bad relationship. The same story goes for misinterpretations. Recall that we indicated that relationships go bad because of what we say to each other – true – but really, most of the time, it is not what you say to the other, it is what interpretation the other draws of what you say. And unfortunately, that interpretation is almost always different from what you meant, and is wrong most of the time. Misunderstandings can either arise out of misinterpretations or independently of them, but both are a by-product of your own thought processes. Your own impressions of others, as per your mental tape, are the real instigators of the nature and type of interpretations you would draw from what others say.

In conclusion, I would like to say that the purpose of this brief discussion was to identify how different thinking modalities can affect our thinking mind and personality profile, and how it can affect, directly or indirectly, the operational framework of our relationships. We are what we think, and that sets the tone for our personality. And since our person-personality is the one that carries on the relationship game, our thinking, therefore, indirectly exerts a profound influence on the harmony of our relationships.

15
ANGER

"Repentance is not a sign of weakness;
It shows that your soul isn't dead yet."

In this chapter, I am going to address the issue of "anger", and its impact on the relationship interplay. Since anger is the nucleus of all antagonistic feelings of hurt that come into play in relationships, its mention is bound to be in continuum throughout the book. Here, I would like to discuss four closely related factors: anger, violence, revenge, and envy, and examine their impact on the relationship interplay.

Anatomy of Anger

Anger is the most destructive and damaging aspect of human emotions. It plays havoc in everything we do in life, but more so in relationships. Anger is all bad – there is absolutely nothing good about it – in whatever form and shape you look at it. Anger can be generated in several different ways, such as:

- A simple routine relationship annoyance can trigger anger. Somebody says something bad to you and both of you know that it is bad or unacceptable – you get irritated and a feeling of indignation and antagonism sets in, which triggers anger. Anger in this case is, indeed, a normal and justifiable response.
- You can derive your own wrong meaning of what somebody says to you and generate a feeling of anger, even when what the other person said had absolutely no bad intentions. This scenario calls for your evaluating your own mental-thinking framework and the nature of your relationship with the other person. Because, either you are negativistic in your attitude, or you have pent-up feelings of anger and antagonism against the person.

- Anger may also be generated purely through your own fantasy — a dangerous form of anger because it is not a by-product of reality. There are two distinct situations in this scenario. First, where someone has said something bad to you, or you feel it was bad, but instead of clarifying the situation with the other person, you go into a fantasy zone where you sit and sulk in silence and generate hypothetical phantoms of anger, antagonism, and revenge. Your inside is mentally fighting with the other person, and you are saying — mentally of course — I hate him — I will hate him until I die — even after death, I will come back to haunt him — I am going to fix him — what does he think of himself — I will show him who and what I am — he doesn't know he is playing with fire — I will teach him the lesson of his life. The second fantasy situation is even more dangerous — where, nobody has said or done anything to you — you create your own fantasy phantom — that the other person "will" or "might" say something bad to you — which may never even happen — but you are generating anger inside you against the person simply through your own mental imagery. Both of these fantasy situations are very dangerous, and they seriously reflect on your own predisposition to anger. They need serious attention and correction for they can devastate and damage any relationship — whether that is marital, or of relatives, or of friends.

- Finally, there is another facet of anger: that inside you, you are, in general, an "angry person". That you are a very negative person by nature — you are unhappy and unfulfilled with life and society. You are always wanting to set the world right — but only to your right — to what you think is right — which, of course, may not be the right right anyway. You get angry with anybody and everybody on anything or everything. This is the virtual worst form of anger, for it leaves no room for reconciliation. Relationships with such a person are always one-sided, the side of "his" right.

Let me tell you a funny, but real, story about "anger". One time, I was driving along to go to a certain place to meet someone. I wasn't sure of the directions to get there. Halfway through, I saw two men standing on the roadside, and I stopped to get directions from them. I opened the car window and asked them: gentlemen! Would you please guide me how to get there? One of the two men spoke up and said: "I don't care where you are going – I don't want you to park your car here". For a minute, I was baffled – but, controlling myself, I humbly repeated by saying: Sir! I am not parking my car – I am only asking for directions. The same man spoke up again, and said the same thing again: "I don't care where you are going – I don't want you to park your car here." Then suddenly, the other man spoke up, and he said to his friend: Stupid! He is not parking his car – he is simply asking you for directions. And this second person gave me excellent directions. I drove away, but for the rest of my journey, I kept thinking about the whole incident, and two things clearly emerged out of my thinking: What a difference between two people – two personalities; what an angry person.

Of all the facets of personality that I have described, and all the reasons emerging out of those that cause relationship problems, anger is the single most important ingredient in all of them. Every scenario of a bad relationship begins with the birth of anger – which then starts accumulating with more and more anger arising out of continuous streak of confrontations – filling the mental-tape to full capacity – and sending the relationship into a spasm. And from where reconciliation and return of harmony is only possible if we eliminate that total build-up of anger from its roots.

Anger is much like stress – it is not lying in wait around the corner to grab you when you pass by, it is something that you generate yourself, by virtue of the personality you have, and this phantom of your creation is not something out there that you can fight – it is all within you. You create it – you hoard it – of your own wanting – therefore, you have to destroy it, by your own effort. And surely that is possible. We shall continue to look for anger-elimination strategies as we move along.

Anger and Violence

Anger and violence are the two faces of the same coin, anger is the inside face – inside you, and violence is the outside face – the outcome of anger. Generally, violence is a by-product of anger. Violence, indeed, is a happening of many relationship scenarios. Although the context of violence is normally via anger, it is important to understand the nature of violence in its own right.

- Anger and violence are, both, attained characteristics, you have to work hard to be violent – because no person is violent by nature – for no one can want pain, and violence is nothing but pain. You become violent because of a reason, whatever the reason may be. The same holds for anger – you don't get angry for nothing – there is always a reason – whether that reason is extrinsic annoyances or intrinsic unhappiness.

- By nature, we are non-violent. That's a given – part of our unconscious self – we don't have to even think about non-violence. That's why it's very hard to define non-violence. The only definition you can give is: non-violence means the absence of violence. But that really means discussing violence. So, in fact, if we need to discuss anything – that is violence – its presence or absence – and, inadvertently, absence turns out to mean non-violence.

- It is much like defining "health". What is health – or what's being healthy – it simply means being not sick. But then that's defining sickness, not health – or trying to define health in terms of sickness. It shows that it's easy to define sickness, violence, or anger – and that's what we should think about – because those are attained entities – they can be "de-attained" also.

- Secondly, violence is accidental – a happening – it's not part of us – for no person can be violent twenty-four hours a day. It's just like no man can be a thief twenty-four hours a day. In fact, a thief steals so that he can save some time for not being a thief, but only a person by himself. He wants to make some money, in some period of time, so that he can enjoy the remainder of the time. The same goes for violence and anger – you can't be violent or angry twenty-four hours a day – it is accidental – it's a happening.

Since violence is a by-product of anger, the first thing we need to do to alleviate violence is to control or eliminate anger. Anger is a man-made emotional response, so if you can control your emotional responses, you can control your anger. All you need to do is to play it incident-by-incident: anger comes – dissipate it – anger goes. Don't let it build or don't even suppress it. A built-up anger makes the mental-tape that destroys the relationship harmony. A suppressed anger is even worse –

the more you suppress it – the more violent it becomes – and ultimately it can open up, almost like a volcano – uncontrollable.

Here is a simple recipe for controlling and dissipating your anger, and I shall use a case scenario to elucidate it. Suppose you are angry with your spouse over something that she said. You are building up your anger, and you are waiting until you reach home from work to vent your anger on her. Stop there, before you reach home. Stop your car on the side of the road. Now, try to act out and play out your anger, as if your spouse is sitting in front of you. Rehearse what you are going to say, and how you are going to get angry when you reach home. When you have done that, you would be surprised how silly you are – you will probably laugh at yourself – how poor an actor you are. Chances are that when you reach home, you won't show or vent your anger. This is called "mindfulness" – this is the "awareness" – the "awakening" – the "inner-evolution". We shall further elaborate on these facets, in the proceeding chapters.

Anger and Revenge

Revenge is a desire to harm the other, and it's generally fuelled by anger. The nature and intensity of revenge varies with the person's own perception of wrongdoing. Revenge is more prevalent in business or friendship relationships – it's virtually non-existent in marital relationships, because in marital relationships, you are so close to each other that harm done to the other really falls back on yourself. Revenge is of two kinds: open and hidden. Although revenge is bad in any form or shape, if it has to be, it's better if it is an "open revenge" – because then it's in the open – and both parties are equally aware of the reasons why it is happening – and there is the hope and possibility of the dissipation of revenge through reconciliation.

Hidden revenge is dangerous because it is not visible, and one cannot assess its intensity, frequency, or permanency. It's a mode that keeps a person engrossed in the cycle of "never-forgetting", and "never-forgiving". Hidden revenge and hidden anger keeps the relationship in a constant state of disorientation because its covertness doesn't allow reconciliation, and possible attempts to correct it or dissipate it go wasted. Just imagine an anger-filled person – continuing with his relationship – while not letting the other person know that he is angry or sore – it's a life-long punishment – it's a perfect recipe for relationship disaster.

Anger and Envy

Finally, we examine the relationship between envy and anger, and see how it affects our relationships. Like revenge, envy is also generally directed to only non-marital-type relationships – that of relatives and friends.

What is envy? Envy is the outcome of unfulfilled desires. When you have a number of desires and you are not able to fulfill them, then a feeling of anger brews inside you, and you direct this anger – as envy – onto another person or persons who have all that you want or more. Envy is generally with regard to money or what money can buy, though in lesser degrees, it can be related to other things such as: envy of others' success, fame, personality, health, wife/husband/children, etc.

Envy is a creation of your own mind, and its root causes are your own desires. And desires can be untenable in two ways: your desires can be illogical and unreasonable, or your desires may be above your capability to fulfill them. So when you can't fulfill your desires, you get frustrated, unhappy, and angry inside, and now you are looking for an avenue to vent your anger. And the easiest prey is the person who has all that you desire, so you become envious of the other person's success and achievements. In fact, there is a high possibility of your becoming envious of the other person's person.

Mentally then, you would want to inflict misfortunes on the person you envy, but unfortunately, envy cannot inflict damage on the person envied – it rather inflicts damage on your own self – and on your relationship with the person. The damage to your own self is in the form of continued unhappiness and a feeling of unfulfillment, which, if continued, can tell upon your self-confidence, self-esteem, and maturity. Instead of deriving pleasure from what he himself has, the envious person creates pain for himself from what others have. The envious person always lives in a competitive and comparative mode of life, and is always comparing with what others have. His own life is not his own, it is pawned to others.

I know of a personal friend who is unfulfilled and he even blames God for not giving him what he wants. Believing in many different forms of God's incarnations – he runs from God to God – praying and hoping that at least one of those many God's incarnations would fulfill all his desires. And when he doesn't get what he wants, which obviously is a reality, he gets angry with God.

Unfulfillment is a curse, and this curse is self-inflicted. The irony of desires is that they are endless in number – when you satisfy one desire, another one takes birth to take its place. There is no vacuum in the domain of desires, and this is how you remain constantly unfulfilled in trying to fulfill all of your desires. Envy is much like worries – there are so many people who are virtually obsessed with worrying – they are the epitome of worries – they must worry all the time – when one worry is over – they start looking for what else to worry about. In fact, they never run short of worries because they can even start worrying about not having something to worry about. This is the personification of unfulfillment – this is human nature.

The problem is that we don't know what we want – or what would make us happy and fulfilled. When we think that we know what we want – and we get it – it is then that we come to realize that that's not what we wanted – and then, we shift our want to something else – and the vicious cycle goes on.

- A housewife is not happy – she wanted to be a workingwoman.
- A working woman is jealous of the ones who have the luxury of staying home.
- A professor wants to be a businessman – a businessman wants to be a professor.

The list for unfulfillment is endless. Personally, I think no one is happy with what they have, or even if they are happy, they still also want something other than what they have, in addition to what they have.

How does it affect our relationships? Well! For a start – envy and unfulfillment make us angry – anger affects our person-personality – which affects our attitude and behavior – which, ultimately, affect the harmony of our relationships. An envious person is generally depressed and angry inside, even when he doesn't show it externally. He always doubts his own capabilities, and always feels a lack of self-confidence. This type of feeling, in fact, adds more fuel to the fire – because the more he feels depressed and unconfident – the more he lacks the ability to achieve what he wants – the more he gets angry and frustrated – the more he envies – and the more he is unhappy in his relationship. It's a catch-22 situation: since you don't have what you desire – you feel incapable – and since you feel incapable – you don't have the energy to achieve what you want.

The only way out is to break through this cycle. And the good news is that, since envy, anger, and fulfillment are man-made entities, they are, therefore, also man-correctable. Here are a few thoughts for a fulfilling life:

- Bring about the awareness in you that you have a feeling of anger, envy, and unfulfillment. Awareness and acceptance is the first most important step forward towards getting rid of your wild desires.

- Keep in mind that God made every single person different (GG1) – and each one of us have different capabilities – different desires – and different levels of fulfillment and success.

- Human nature, fortunately, has another compensating passion – namely, that of "admiration". Why don't you utilize this ability, and replace your envy of others by your admiration of others' achievements – you will feel profoundly satisfied, happy, and fulfilled inside you.

- When something pleasant happens – stop and enjoy that moment to the fullest extent possible – rather than complaining that it could have been better.

- Enjoy what you have rather than worrying about what you don't have or what others have. Be thankful to God – first – for what He has given you – before you complain for what He hasn't given you.

- Live in the present – live your own life – not that of others.

16
FANTASY

"The mind personifies love;
The heart feels it;
The soul purifies it."

The subject of fantasy, in general, is indeed very broad. So for the sake of focused brevity, I would limit my discussion to the marital-type fantasies only — and that too only in the context of how it affects the health of our relationships. Marital fantasies — it's a very sensitive topic indeed — not too many people openly discuss it or speak about it. Yet I believe that because it is real — because it is quite prevalent — and because it does, directly or indirectly, impact the harmony and health of our relationships — it is important to clearly understand it. Basically, I am interested in the following three aspects:

- What is spousal fantasy?
- Why does it arise?
- How does it affect our relationships?

What is spousal fantasy? Well! It's not that easy to define, nor is it as easy to encapsulate into a single sentence. Still, as a first cut — and an over-simplified one — I would define it as follows:

"Spousal fantasy is a process through which you
fulfill some kind of unfulfilled physical desires
through mental imagery."

Fantasy, as you may realize, is a mental process — so its fulfillment has to be a mental one, not an actual verbatim physical one — even when the onset of mental imagery may be because of some physical entity. A thought is a thought — it can rarely arise without a reason — howsoever small or insignificant the reason may be. Deep down in your psyche, there may be a desire that may be unfulfilled — partially or wholly — and fantasy provides an easy means of harmlessly realizing it — on a mental platform, of course. Mind is a very fertile entity, so the range of fantasies can be very broad. It can be a simple titillation of the mental imagery to satisfy a harmless desire or it can be a serious thought to satisfy an actual physical and emotional unfulfilled desire.

To understand the nature of spousal fantasies, I would first attempt to highlight some obvious categories of spousal fantasies:

- **Category 1**: Fantasies that are directed to your own spouse only – for greater physical and emotional fulfillment.
- **Category 2**: Fantasies that are directed to someone other than your own spouse – but only as a means to enhance and achieve greater physical and emotional fulfillment with your own spouse.
- **Category 3**: Fantasies that may be directed by both of you together to something that you both mutually enjoy – in order to enhance your collective love and togetherness.
- **Category 4**: Fantasies that are directed to someone other than your own spouse – as a means of emotional fulfillment that you, seemingly, don't achieve from your own spouse.

The Need for a Fantasy

Why do spousal fantasies arise? Typically, I think fantasies arise because of some unfulfilled desires, whatever their nature or intensity. These desires may be fully evident to you or they may be hidden deep down in your psyche – and all you feel is that there is something missing – something is not fulfilled. You feel a void inside you, and a lack of contentment. And this type of vacuum can come into being with any of the following two situations:

- When your relationship is okay, but there is a feeling of something amiss.
- When a crack occurs in your relationship, and a feeling of dissension sets in.

Let's now elaborate on the four categories of fantasies identified above.

Category 1: Fantasies directed to your own spouse – this category connotes a healthy form of fantasy, for it is directed to your own spouse only. Though I think, at times, it may be important to still analyze it – just to find out what kind of desires you have that are unfulfilled, and for which the need for fantasy has arisen – because, after all, if there is no unfulfilled desire, then why should the need for fantasy arise in the first place. Notwithstanding however, this aspect of fantasy is positive in nature and it can surely help in accentuating your togetherness.

Category 2: Fantasies directed to someone other than your own spouse. For this category, I want to present some hypothetical fantasy scenarios:

A married man may generally fantasize the following:

- I wish my wife were as beautiful as Brenda.
- I wish my wife would give me more love – like other wives do.
- I wish my wife cared for me and my feelings and needs – more than she does.

A married woman may generally fantasize the following:

- I wish my husband were as tall and handsome as Robert.
- I wish my husband loved and cared for me as much as Steve does for his wife.
- I wish my husband behaved more pleasantly, and would listen to me more than he does.

This is, indeed, just a sample of things that both sexes may fantasize about – there is no limit to what we can fantasize about – the sky is the limit. This category is part healthy, and part not so healthy. It is healthy to the extent that its result is directed only to your own spouse, and its purpose is also noble – to enhance your love and togetherness with your spouse. The unhealthy part is that it may be indicative of a crack occurring in the relationship, and can have the distinct possibility to make you go astray. As a minimum, this type of fantasy thinking can generate some unhealthy feelings, such as:

- That your own spouse is deficient in some ways
- That your own spouse is unable to provide you with complete physical and/or emotional fulfillment
- That you do have some unfulfilled desires hidden deep inside you.

Category 3: Mutual fantasies – this is where you and your spouse both – jointly and mutually – fantasize about something – to enhance your love and togetherness. For the most part, it's a healthy form of fantasy, and it can certainly invigorate your love. But unfortunately, it can also create a disastrous situation if the relationship goes bad. For example, if your relationship goes sour in the "Dinner phase", your spouse may turn around and start digging the past, and may start blaming you for those fantasies, and may even start accusing you of dishonesty and betrayal – even when those fantasies were done together and with mutual consent. At that juncture, there is a risk that you may be swayed away from your spouse.

Category 4: Fantasies directed to the other – this category of fantasies signals the onset of a rupture in your relationship, and an indication that you no longer derive physical or emotional fulfillment from each other – this is the worst of all scenarios.

Whenever a mishap of annoyance or dissent happens in a relationship, whatever its nature or intensity, a certain feeling of distance sets in between the husband and the wife – a vague feeling of repulsion and anger. It may be very mild in nature, and it may be only just inside you – unspoken and silent. The physical fulfillment – which is a product of full, complete, and undeterred mutual togetherness – also takes a direct hit. Along with it, its close cousin – emotional fulfillment – also takes a hit. A process begins – the process of faint fantasies – for the satisfaction of physical fulfillment – via mental imagery – for the ultimate satisfaction of emotional fulfillment. As the relationship discord widens, so does the circle of fantasies.

And, speaking of "emotional fulfillment" – typically, it is a non-existent entity by itself, because it is not on a physical plain – it is only a mental realization. Therefore, we have to search for the source – where it comes from – and that source is "physical fulfillment" – which is on a plain of actual physical happenings. As such therefore, emotional fulfillment is a by-product of physical fulfillment. Consequently, the onset of fantasy is the unfulfillment of physical desires, which may include: love, care, compassion, or any other pertinent aspect of life and living – which ultimately contributes to emotional fulfillment.

But, physical unfulfillment generally sets in when a hairline crack develops in a relationship, and consequently, that's also the starting point of the process of fantasy. And since fulfillment is a necessity of life – you begin to go astray – away from your own spouse – and wander around for fulfillment. Initially, that fulfillment may only be at the mental plain – via mental imagery, but it has the possibility of going out, physically, with others, out of the context of your own spouse.

With this discussion, I think we can now appreciate how different fantasy modes can affect our relationship. My own premise is that, although fantasies arise out of unfulfilled physical desires, it is really the emotional unfulfillment that is the key to the whole drama. In studying many a cases, I have come to observe that even when physical fulfillment is complete – many a couples still remain emotionally unfulfilled – especially in bad relationships. Which tells me that – it's really more important to direct your attention to emotional unfulfillment to see how that can be appropriately satisfied.

Emotional Fulfillment and Fantasy

Emotional fulfillment comes through mental fulfillment, and both are a matter of the mind. They are not on a physical plain – they are a creation of the mind. If mental fulfillment cannot be achieved through physical fulfillment – then how can it be fulfilled through fantasy? And, if fantasy does fulfill it, it clearly means that fulfillment is a matter of the mind – a state created by the mind. Which means that if we wish, we can fulfill ourselves simply by our mental thoughts – we don't need any external stimulus – whether it be fantasy or actual physical entities. We can be fulfilled in as little as nothing, if we want to, or remain perpetually and continuously unfulfilled, even if we have everything that we ever wanted to have. If unfulfillment becomes a permanent mode of your thinking, then you will always remain unfulfilled even if you get all that you want. Fantasy is a road with no end – when one fantasy is satisfied, another one takes birth – and we get busy in satisfying that – and this endless cycle continues.

Take, for example, the case of the wife who fantasizes for a tall and handsome man, like Robert. Even if she gets what she wants, she would still fantasize – now perhaps, for some other characteristics than "tall and handsome". By the way, all she needs to do is to check with Robert's wife to see if she is happy with Robert – the tall and handsome man. In all probability – no – Robert's wife may be happy with the characteristics of "tall and handsome", but she may be miserable because the tall and handsome husband is also unpleasant, or at times, even unfaithful.

Take the case of the husband – he may find Brenda to be more beautiful than his own wife, but Brenda may be worthless in all other characteristics of personality, in which his own wife is very good.

More weird! Even if we have the opportunity and control to get a custom-made spouse, I am very sure that we will still complain – still be dissatisfied – will still fantasize.

What does fantasy do to us – it keeps our mind continually engrossed in silent unfulfillment, and perhaps, even in silent anger and frustration. There is a constant void and vacuum in your mind, life, and relationship, that doesn't let you realize or maintain the fullness and pleasantness of your current relationship.

Fantasies, out of context of your current relationships – slowly and systematically destroy the internal harmony of your relationship – because fantasy keeps increasing the distance between your togetherness – and consequently, it keeps throwing you into silent separations, unhappy relationships – which ultimately may even break. What you need to understand is that fantasy is an outcome of unfulfillment – and unfulfillment is simply caused by relationship discord. Therefore, fantasy is not a cure for fulfillment – relationship harmony is – and you need to reconcile and generate a permanent sense of harmony in your relationship.

Actually, if you must fantasize, fantasize about each other or mutually and jointly together for something. This would enhance your relationship harmony and continually invigorate your love and togetherness.

Here is a beautiful scenario for you – following is a note that a husband sent to his wife when he had gone on an assignment – and was fantasizing about her:

> "You are my Rose"
> I am like a Rose tree;
> You are the Rose on that tree;
> Without you – the Rose;
> I am not a Rose tree;
> I am just a tree;
> With branches full of leaves and thorns;
> You make me the Rose tree;
> You are the genesis of my existence.

How beautiful!!!

17
EXPECTATIONS

"Flowers don't live in the past or the future;
Flowers live in the present.
Be a flower."

In this chapter, I want to elaborate on another behavioral characteristic — "Expectations" — but at the same time, I also want to consider the issue of possessiveness, which is an offshoot of expectations. Both of these characteristics bear influence on the harmony of our relationships. The characteristic of "expectation" is more applicable to relative-type relationships, whereas that of "possessiveness" is more commonly associated with marital-type relationships. I would keep my discussion short, because all I want to do is pinpoint another characteristic that can influence our relationship interaction.

Anatomy of Expectations

What is an expectation? Basically, an expectation is something that you would like the other person to do for you, and it can be a mental or behavioral desire, or it can be a physical need. Whatever it is — it is still an imposition on the other — and its impact on your relationship is directly proportional to how you perceive its fulfillment. There are two ways you can look at its fulfillment — as your inherent right, or as a prerogative of the other. Relationships may not break directly and abruptly because of a single unfulfilled expectation, but they can certainly break or go into permanent limbo with the cumulative effect of many unfulfilled expectations over time.

Expectations come in varying sizes and shapes — pleasant, fair, genuine, humble, trivial — on one end; exorbitant, untenable, unfair, impossible — on the other end. But whatever their intent, they can exert a profound influence on our relationship harmony. Although expectations put a heavy emotional burden on both parties — one who is expecting, and the other who is being expected from – the one who is being expected from suffers a much greater brunt and strain from unfulfilled expectations.

It is, indeed, true that expectations are a necessary and integral part of our life and relationships – for in the circle of relatives, there is surely nothing wrong in expecting something from a loved one, because after all, if you cannot expect something from someone you love, who else can you expect from. In that sense – yes, expectations are a sign of love, trust, and respect. Still however, when expectations exceed their threshold of fairness, they become a constant source of anger, botheration and frustration.

An easy way to understand this dilemma is to examine the difference between the expectations of a friend and those of a relative. In friendship, an expectation would be like a humble request – if it gets fulfilled – fine; if not – there may be a temporary soreness – but the relationship is unlikely to break because of that. The expectations within the circle of relatives plays havoc because there is a definitive connotation of "birth-right" – "relationship-right" – with a pressure that it must be fulfilled. I am your mother – I am your brother – I am your wife – I am your brother-in-law – if I can't ask you to do something for me, then who else can I ask – if you can't do this little thing for me, then what worth is our relationship. It's a do-or-die situation – we are ready to sacrifice our relationship at the altar of expectations. Under the veil of the fifth commandment – "the right" – so much emotional blackmail goes on among relatives to get their expectations satisfied – all in the name of being a relative. Surely, as a relative, you have a right to expect, but do relatives ever examine the nature and intensity of their expectations, over and above being a "right", to see if their expectations are viable and possible for the person to fulfill? Most likely never – and that is precisely the root cause of relationship problems among relatives.

Think of a situation where you would like your brother to fulfill your expectation – be it a physical need or a mental whim – and now contemplate on the following:

- Firstly, it's your desire or need – not your brother's – you should try to fulfill it yourself – for why should your brother fulfill something that is exclusively yours and not his. Or, if you can't fulfill it because it is too stringent, then reduce its complexity and try fulfilling it now. And, if it is just impossible for you to fulfill it yourself, then you should not generate such desires in the first place, for they can create the same annoyance and difficulty for your brother.

- If you still need help, then at least assess the validity, intensity, and viability of your need vis-à-vis the circumstances, capabilities, and wishes of your brother – to see if he can help you.

- But, even if you want your brother to help you – it has to be a request – not your right – it has to be your brother's prerogative, whether he wishes to help or not. You cannot make a complaint if he doesn't help, and if he does, you have to be thankful.

- Lastly, it's very important that you should always carefully evaluate the factual viability and reasonableness of your desires and expectations before you extend them to your brother. In the same token, you should also keep in mind your brother's capability as well as his desire to fulfill.

This brief description should at least give you an indication that relationship interactions can be plagued by untenable expectations, and therefore, you should exercise control and good judgment over your desires and expectations of others.

Expectations and Possessiveness

"Possessiveness" or "ownership", when combined with untenable expectations, can cause serious relationship problems. Ownership of objects is understandable, but when you extend your desires and expectations of possessiveness onto people – that's where relationship problems occur. Anytime we extend our expectations onto a relative, we tend to, intentionally or unintentionally, attach the connotation of "relationship-right" or "relationship-possessiveness" along with that expectation. Our expectations are loaded with ownership of the relative, and consequently, their fulfillment becomes an obsession.

Possessiveness is a desire to own the other – in the context that the other should be doing what you think best. In the name of relationships – to some extent – this desire and gesture is justifiable, but only as a mutually operable and acceptable entity. When it goes beyond the threshold of mutual respect and mutual concurrence – then it becomes an obsession, and it begins to affect the relationship.

Let me now, for the sake of brevity, limit my discussion of possessiveness to only the marital-type relationship, and examine how this relationship is affected by this behavioral tendency. For a marital relationship, possessiveness is the anti-thesis of the basic precept upon which the relationship was built in the first place. A marital relationship is built on the premise that we two will live together and care for each other – but only as long as we have the freedom to maintain our self-identity and self-recognition. Despite this, unfortunately, possessiveness is a disease that prevalently affects marital relationships.

Why do we want to possess others? Perhaps because we don't own ourselves, and we want to compensate our internal weakness through an external achievement. You cannot satisfy internal weakness through external ownership – its like satisfying hunger or thirst through the eyes, rather than through the mouth. Internal poverty cannot be eliminated through external wealth.

What happens when you start possessing your spouse – to the extent of "suffocating possessiveness"? Intuitively, you are trying to kill the spouse's self-identity – or in other words, you are trying to kill her – reduce her to meaninglessness. And how do you do this – by imposing emotional rules and principles. The simple fact of possessiveness is that – you simply cannot possess the other without killing the other. A living person cannot be possessed, because he upholds his self-identity. So what happens in the process of possessing the other – the husband starts killing the wife – and the wife starts killing the husband – howsoever unknowingly and unintentionally. And they do not rest until the other person is dead. And here is the funniest of all enigmas – when the other is dead, we feel there is no charm left in life, because what's the fun of living with a dead person.

What a paradox – until the spouse is dead – we remain worried – and when she dies – we are unhappy. Remember! We are speaking of "possessiveness-death", not "absolute-death". And what do we do now – that's where the journey into the land of fantasy starts – that's where the relationship cracks begin to appear. We may start looking for somebody else – other than our spouse – somebody who is not dead – why – because we want to associate with somebody who is alive, not dead – even when we killed our spouse ourselves.

146

The man may, for example, start looking for another girlfriend because the wife is dead – and the other woman can now, seemingly, provide that emotional fulfillment, which his own wife could not provide – because she is dead – all hypothetical imagery and fantasy anyway.

Why is the other woman more attractive – because he has not possessed her yet – he hasn't killed her yet? But the day the girlfriends become the wife – the process of ownership will start all over again – and it won't be too long before the new wife is dead also. And then we start looking for more non-dead bodies – and the cycle goes on. So, you can see what the obsession of ownership does to a relationship over time.

Notwithstanding however, there are ownerships that can also be very rewarding:
- Ownership of the self – knowing who you are – what you are.
- Ownership of the other – with mutual respect and dignity – a prime ingredient for a happy and healthy relationship. Ownership of each other – of mutual respect and love in a marital relationship is very important.

Any other type of ownership is nothing but pain. It is not only the person owned who is miserable, the owner himself is perhaps even more miserable. The master of a slave is more miserable than the slave itself.

Happy and healthy relationships are built on:
- Mutual respect
- Mutual recognition
- Love

The desire and expectation of possessiveness cancels out the mutual respect and recognition – and makes "love" a one-sided option – receiving, but not giving. Make your ownership of the other a matter of sharing love and respect.

18
FULFILLMENT

"When you become one in love;
Giving and taking becomes the same."

Although, in general, I have spoken enough about this very important facet of our life – "fulfillment" – all through the book, I wish to close this section with a few final thoughts about "fulfillment". Personal fulfillment is, perhaps, the end-all goal of every person. Everything that we do – all of our efforts, actions, and the run-around of life – they are all geared to achieving things we desire – by virtue of which we fulfill ourselves. The desires may come in different sizes and shapes for each individual, yet the ultimate goal is the fulfillment of those desires.

What is fulfillment? Fulfillment is that inner satisfaction – a feeling of success and achievement – a feeling of contentment – a feeling of happiness. Fulfillment is a very elusive entity because it is not a fixed and stationary entity; it's a moving target. Fulfillment is a by-product of fulfilled desires, but desires can hardly be completely fulfilled – which means complete fulfillment is not possible – it is a hypothetical entity. Why can't desires be fulfilled – because desires are always open-ended – they are endless in quantity and quality – and since they are never-ending, their fulfillment is never-ending? The only way out of this vicious circle is to realize that fulfillment – being a man-made entity – is a matter of the mind. You can be fulfilled with almost nothing – or you may be unfulfilled even if you have everything you ever wanted to have.

It's always a conflict between "being" and "having" – and unfortunately, "having" cannot be transformed into "being" – unless you don't let your desires overpower your fulfillment. The race for achieving your desires is endless – because your desires are endless. Once you have achieved one desire – it gives birth to the next desire – there is no void in the domain of desires. Consequently, once you have fulfilled one desire, the process brings you back to the starting point again – and the race starts all over again. Endless desires – endless race – endless unfulfillment.

Endless unfulfillment is catastrophic for relationships. Unlike other traits, such as aggressiveness, egoism, immaturity, and the righteousness syndrome, which have a direct impact on the happiness of our relationship, fulfillment also exerts a significant impact, but indirectly. A feeling of fulfillment brings in a sense of stability, calmness, satisfaction, and happiness. Consequently, a contented and happy person would, naturally, be more positive and friendly – and would have better and happier relationships.

Fulfillment can be broadly classified into three categories: Physical, Material, and Emotional (mental). The ultimate goal for us all is "emotional fulfillment". The physical and material fulfillment are components of the ultimate goal, and they collectively contribute to the greater goal, that of "emotional fulfillment".

Physical Fulfillment

This relates to the physical self – what you are as you are – your appearance – your health – your total physical well-being – which can, indirectly, affect your mental well-being, emotional fulfillment, behavior, and hence your relationship interactions. Notwithstanding, since physical fulfillment is a matter of mental acceptance, you should try to make feasible amendments and improvements in the physical aspects of your life to achieve physical as well as mental fulfillment.

Material Fulfillment

Material fulfillment is the mainframe of our life and living, and as such, it exerts a profound influence on our behavior, maturity, and general fulfillment. Two important facets of material fulfillment are: Money and Recognition. The fulfillment of both of these goals imparts a feeling of euphoric satisfaction and happiness, and a person in that state of emotional fulfillment is bound to be happy with himself, as well as with his relationships.

Speaking of money as a goal – I think it is a very important goal – it enters into the scene in two ways:

- Money as a basic need – physical fulfillment
- Money as a mental desire – emotional fulfillment.

Undeniably, money is a fundamental necessity for carrying out and maintaining the basic framework of life. For example – love, happiness, and compassion – they are all very important – yet there is very little chance that you will think about those if you don't have the basic financial security and means to survive and live. What is the basic need of a desperate and starving person – food and money – not mental happiness – which, of course, may come, but only when the stomach is full? It is a widely known fact that a lot of times, a lack of money is the main source of discontentment and fights in a family's relationship. A husband and wife with a desperate shortage of money are, generally, more stressed out and irritable with each other. The financial strain generally causes depression, anger, and a sense of failure – and all of these factors play havoc on day-to-day relationship harmony. Fulfillment of this basic need is, therefore, fundamental to the continued happiness of a relationship.

Money as a mental desire is, more or less, a part of the desire domain. And since desires can be endless – the money range can be endless. It's rather a question of mind over matter, and you can certainly exercise control to be fulfilled, even without the obsessive money desire.

The second element is the desire for "recognition" – we all have that hunger for praise and accolade – recognition for self-esteem and for self-righteousness.

Emotional Fulfillment

I have introduced this category simply because of its profound interplay and impact on relationships, especially in the context of a marital relationship. Personally I believe that in a marital relationship, even when we are continuously seeking physical and material fulfillment, our real goal is "emotional fulfillment". Our relationships go bad – or remain in silent separations – or remain unfulfilled – merely because we remain emotionally unfulfilled.

Here is a new thought that would highlight the importance of emotional fulfillment. Take the case of infidelity – even when we get physical and mental fulfillment from our own spouse, we still run around for somebody else – why – because of our craving for emotional fulfillment. There is an imbalance of emotional feelings on the mental-tape for our spouse, and despite all the physical fulfillments available to us, we still go out to look for emotional fulfillment – whether we get it or not is, again, a matter of mind over matter. And speaking about "mind over matter" – emotional fulfillment is also a matter of "mind over matter" – it is also a matter of our imagination – something of our own making. We can easily achieve emotional fulfillment through mental control and satisfaction if we want to.

In conclusion – fulfillment is absolutely important – a fulfilled person is a happy person. A happy person is a pleasant person and will, in all probability, generate happy relationships. Fulfillment comes through acceptance of what you are and what you have. That, of course, doesn't mean relinquishing your desires, especially viable and necessary desires. It simply means that you exercise complete control over your desires, evaluate the need for their fulfillment, and then go after them one step at a time. The point is that you control the process – without letting the process control you.

Incidentally, I have a beautiful scenario that I would like to recount. Robert is a good friend, but whenever we sit together, Robert starts complaining about his life and living – about things that he doesn't have and wished he had. One day, I couldn't control myself, and I asked Robert to go along with me to answer a few questions that I would like to ask about his unfulfillment. This is how our conversation went:

- Robert – do you have a good job?
- Yes, indeed – I am very happy with my job – it pays quite well.
- Robert – are you basically healthy?
- Yes – I am quite healthy – I have no serious ailment.
- Robert – is you wife nice?
- Yes, couldn't ask for a better woman.
- Robert – is your house paid for?
- Yes – most of the mortgage has been paid for – I am almost debt-free.
- Robert – are you financially secure and sound?
- Not only secure and sound – I think I am pretty well off.
- Robert – do you normally and routinely travel, have holidays, eat out, and enjoy life.
- I think I have the best of all worlds.

I stopped there, and suddenly asked Robert – if that's what you have – then what are you complaining about. You have everything that you want – how come you feel so unfulfilled. Robert was totally bewildered and answerless – he didn't realize what I was trying to do, and where I was leading him. I was a bit afraid that Robert would get angry with me – but luckily, it didn't happen. In fact, on the contrary – and to my surprise – Robert was thankful to me for opening his eyes. He says he feels more fulfilled now – and I seriously hope he does.

It's a silly little example, but scenarios like this do highlight a few important messages for us. That we are unhappy with our own being, with what we are and what we have – and that our unhappiness is our own creation.

Typically, what do we want:
- John's money
- Steve's wife
- Dick's health
- Jim's house
- Doug's business success
- Robert's academic intelligence
- Roger's children

And the list is endless. What we have is no good – and what we want is the best of everything put together. And I can virtually bet on it that if you get all those things, you would still be as unhappy and unfulfilled as ever.

And there is a further irony, if I ask you "are you unhappy" – you will virtually jump from your seat and categorically and aggressively deny the fact that you are unhappy – even when you are – and even when it's a figment of your imagination. And this is not because you don't want to tell me the truth – you won't even tell it to your own self, if you ask this question to yourself. This is the dilemma of non-reconciliation of unfulfillment – the drama of mind over matter. So, in closing the chapter, the best I can say is that:
- Personal fulfillment is a self-created entity – it is mind over matter.
- Unfulfillment generates an unhappy person-personality – and that hurts your relationships.

SECTION 4
QUANTUM LEAP
THE AWAKENING

19
AWAKENINGS AND INNER-EVOLUTION

"When walking in a relationship – you fall – you get hurt;
But that doesn't mean you stop walking."

With the conclusion of section 3, we have almost completed the "knowledge acquisition" phase. As per our new paradigm, we confirmed that it is not the modes and mediums of behavior, but the person himself – who is responsible for the makings and breakings of relationships. We also propounded that a person is simply a sum total of his personality, and consequently, we studied the personality factors that make the person the "person" he is. Now we have two tasks at hand – first: to find out how to control and amend the impact of various personality factors on our behavior for the sake of maintaining harmonious relationships; and second: to be prepared for the new reconciliation process. These tasks can be encapsulated under the following categories:

- The Awakenings
- The Inner-Evolution

"Awakenings" means – waking up our inner conscious-level awareness of our own total self – and of others in relation to the self – and developing a strong desire to enhance the self. "Inner-Evolution" means – waking up a revolution inside us, and putting our understanding to action in order to achieve total relationship harmony. The total task comprises the following:

- Awareness of self: knowing your self – your total personality profile – and factors that affect your behavior in relationships.
- Acceptance: acceptance of your shortcomings – and willingness to change.
- Awareness of the other: knowing and accepting the other's personality profile.
- Passion for togetherness: being ready for reconciliation to restore harmony.

The main ingredient in the equation of Awakenings and Inner-Evolution is "introspective thinking" – a process of "self-talk" – a process that each partner undergoes on their own – to speak to the self – to analyze the rights and wrongs of their own actions. The process helps to awaken each partner, individually – making them more conducive to mutual reconciliation. The most ideal thing to do is to carry out an introspective analysis after every interaction or confrontation, on a daily basis. Regarding the method of introspection – my preferred method of introspection is via "walking" – going on long and slow walks, for the sake of thinking only – and they must be done alone. In these somnolent walkings – you can talk to yourself freely and honestly – can go over your actions and modes of behavior with others, and can assess your rights and wrongs. This would provide you with greater awakening, maturity, and strength to enhance relationship harmony. And when you have reached a point where you have good control over your own actions, then you can go together and amicably discuss the issues together that impede the flow of harmony in the relationship.

Now let's examine the four steps listed above: awareness of the self, acceptance, awareness of the other, and passion to reconcile.

Awareness of the Self

There are two ways by which you can accomplish this task:

- **Through self-introspection:** Through introspection, you need to examine your own personality profile and evaluate, as judiciously as possible, your shortcomings, and see how they affect your behavior. Try to rate your deficiencies on a severity scale of: high, medium, and low seriousness on each of the personality traits outlined in Section 3. Once you have prioritized them, then you can begin the modification process, starting with the ones that have low seriousness. Suppose, the factor "expectations" is on the low end of seriousness. Study your behavior pattern on how your level of expectations from others affects your relationship. Come to terms with yourself and discuss the matter as follows: firstly, see if your expectations are untenable and justifiable; then pacify yourself by the thoughts that – what will happen if your expectations are not fulfilled – would the heaven fall down? Make every issue a non-challenging affair and you would feel calm and relieved of the unwanted stress that you have been carrying over about that issue. Continuing like this, introspect about each issue like this until you have cleared away most of the issues bothering you. There would still be some issues that you would have to discuss with your partner jointly.

- **In conjunction with your spouse:** A better way to bring about the awareness of the self is to do this exercise jointly with your spouse, if you two have good rapport with each other. In this scenario, each of you would prepare two lists: one with what you think of your spouse, and the other with what you think of your own self – for all important personality characteristics. Once again, create, for each trait, an intensity scale, such as: high, medium, and low seriousness. Now, between the two of you, you should have a total of four lists – and these are to be used for your joint discussion – for understanding your own self and the other, and for bringing the necessary personality changes in order to achieve eternal mutual togetherness and happiness.

The Acceptance

A difficult phase because acceptance can be taken as a sign of weakness and defeat – something that our arrogant ego finds hard to accept. But that would have to be done, because nothing can happen without acceptance of the status quo – you cannot hope to correct something that you don't know or won't accept. Both parties have to do that. The process is not difficult – it just needs you to humble yourself down momentarily and exercise control over your ego-pride. And remember, you are doing it for each other – for your love and happiness.

The Awareness of the Other

Because you need two to play the relationship game, it is vitally important to know: how others feel, their sensitivity threshold, their behavioral patterns, their strengths and weaknesses – in fact, their total personality profile. Give others the respect that you would give to your own self – as if the other is not really the other, but you, across the mirror.

The Passion

Nothing can be accomplished without a personal passion and determination. And this passion can only come from within. The external intervention may help in awakening the dormant inner energy and desire, but that can only happen when you have the inner passion in the first place – for external help acts only as a catalyst. Inner-evolution is an inner thing – something private and inner to you – it is a process of bringing changes in your self by your self – and this process of union with the self starts with you. It is almost mandatory to know the self – for if you don't even know your own self, how can you know the other – and how can you create union either with the self or with the other.

The final equation, therefore, is: know the self; accept the self; amend the self; know the other; respect the other's unique identity; prepare yourself for the new reconciliation.

20

THE STORY OF ADAM AND EVE

"Marriage has a circular relationship;
You marry the person you love;
You love the person you marry."

Marital or marital-type relationships are the nucleus of our life and living — everything emanates from and merges into this relationship. Marriage is a life-game between two people — two personalities — different from each other and yet trying to make it the same. Unlike any other game, this game has either two winners or two losers.

As we have seen in previous discussions — the role-play of men and women — the differences and similarities of the two sexes — plays a crucial role in relationships. So what I want to do is pick up some common scenarios of marital relationships and examine them in the context of our new paradigm to see how adequately our new concepts would fit and how they would provide a better understanding of relationship problems than our current understanding. Although the scenarios that I am considering have already been discussed before, in one form or another, from this treatment, you would be able to see and learn about the actual application of the new perspective to various relationship situations, and also be able to see the appropriateness, uniqueness, and viability of the new concepts. For that matter, this chapter is a test chapter.

Before I begin with specific case scenarios, I would like to go to the beginnings of the marital relationship, and follow through its normal course from the makings to the silent separations or breakings, or perhaps, up to the remakings and reconciliation. Our aim is twofold: one, to understand what forces drive its makings; and two, to understand what idiosyncrasies lead to its breakings. Let's recapitulate our previous description regarding the compartmentalization of our life span into the three phases: the Breakfast, the Lunch, and the Dinner phase.

In the Breakfast phase, we are mostly busy in three things: achieving awareness of the self; establishing self-identity, that is: me, myself as distinctly different and unique from you, yourself; and establishing relationships. Around the end of the Breakfast period and the beginning of the Lunch phase, we are ready to start the process of partnership – forming marital-type relationships.

Incidentally, and sadly enough, as I mentioned earlier – while this is the starting point of the makings of marital relationships, it is also, perhaps unconsciously and unintentionally – the beginning of the breakings of the relationships, because a large majority of marital relationships suffer their demise in the first four to seven years of their makings. As a simple simile, the process of relationships is much like the process of life itself. While the birth is the beginning of life, it is also the beginning of the process of death, for the moment you are born, the countdown to death begins. Normally, we are not consciously aware of this fact – that the beginnings of the makings of this relationship are also the beginnings of its breakings – nor do we want to know, or have any conscious-level desire or intention of its breakings at the time of its makings. We don't make the relationship with a clear intentional knowledge, understanding, or assumption of breaking it – in fact, on the contrary – these relationships are built on beautiful dreams – for a life-long partnership.

So, let us first examine the underlying basis of the makings of this relationship. The best answer I can give you is that – it is the human "need": need to love and be loved; need for procreation; need for companionship; and all other needs of life and living. So that means, while establishing this relationship, at about the Lunch phase, we are, really and truly, accepting the following premise:

- That, I have a clear "awareness" of my "self", and have a distinct "identity"
- That, I accept the fact that my spouse has a distinct "identity"
- That, I am ready for togetherness – "two-getherness"
- That, while respecting the two "identities", I am ready to share my love

Wow! How romantic and beautiful the beginning is! Then what happened to the relationship that was supposedly built on dreams, flowers, and honey – where did it go wrong – why did it start falling apart? This is the big question.

How does the process of breakings start? It starts with feelings:

- Feelings that you are losing your identity by sharing
- Feelings that you are different
- Feelings that your perspective is changing
- Feelings of boredom, emptiness, and soul-weariness creeping in silently
- Feelings that the other is still the other – and not of you – heart and soul
- Feelings of fantasy and comparativeness – that others are better than your own spouse, and you deserved more – more and better than what you got

And when feelings like this creep into the bedroom, the relationship starts its downward deterioration journey, and suddenly the doors of relationship harmony open wide for any eventuality. The eventualities can range from constant bickering and naggings to fighting, with the relationship ending, either in silent separations or breakings. When the relationship reaches this stage, harmonization is only possible if timely action is taken to reconcile the differences – otherwise, the relationship can slowly creep towards deterioration and ultimate disintegration. If, at this stage, you can exercise your better judgment, and you are able to recognize that your relationship is moving towards breakdown, you may be able to save it.

How do you recognize the signs and signals of an impending breakdown? Well! I have a simple formula that I can share with you. If you can just give me ten minutes with a couple – during their conversation – I can guesstimate, with a fairly high degree of accuracy, the state of health of their relationship. Their marriage is, generally, on the rocks if:

- They continuously evade each other or emotionally withdraw from the conversation.
- For the most part, they are complaining and whining.
- They routinely criticize and oppose each other's viewpoint and judgment – defending and protecting their own viewpoints instead.
- Their conversation is largely negativistic, and they perpetually manifest negativistic bodily gestures – like rolling their eyes or frowning.

- They tend to become either neutral and indifferent to each other (turning away), or negativistic (turning against), or they emotionally withdraw from each other.
- They pretend they are listening to each other when they are not.
- They attack each other's character, integrity, and sound judgment.
- In short, you can sense a feeling of unseen, silent repulsion between them.

With this premise, let's now turn our attention to examine some case scenarios to see how and why the relationship reaches the point of disintegration or degeneration. I would like to consider the following six scenarios:

1. Personality differences
2. Identity and co-dependence
3. Mental tape
4. Change of perspective
5. Ego-Sensitivity verses Feelings-Sensitivity
6. Love

1. Personality Differences

The first and the foremost realization that hits you hard in the first few years after marriage, and which changes the tone of your relationship, is the feeling that "you two are two different persons". The honeymoon is over – the reality is dawning – and you are beginning to feel that you two have very different personalities. You differ in almost everything: your thinking – your behavior – your likes and dislikes – you expectations of the self and of each other – in fact, your whole perspective on life is different.

And this feeling is bothering you because it shatters those dreams on which you built your relationship in the first place – the dream that you have found a partner who has the same vibrations as you have. As a matter of fact, you spent so many precious years in courtship to find a partner who is like you – thinks like you – feels like you – behaves like you – has the same interests and tastes as you have. And you found one – or perhaps, you thought you found one – and voila – you got married. And suddenly now, this silent feeling is creeping inside you that you two are two different people.

I am sorry to tell you that it's all your own fault anyway. I think you forgot about my GG1 – "Variety" that I outlined in Chapter 9 – that "God made everyone different". If you knew about GG1, then you would have realized that you were looking for "sameness" in "differentness", which is an inherent impossibility. How could you think that your desires could supersede the will of the Lord?

Perhaps even when you knew that every person is different, you were not intentionally manifesting this reality to each other, because the forces of nature were forcing you to establish and consummate the relationship. Irrespective, you were building a relationship on false assumptions or make-believe assumptions of sameness, and now when reality is catching up with you to make you realize that you two are different – you are getting frustrated in your relationship.

Had you started your relationship with a clear understanding and acceptance of the fact that we are all different, your relationship would still have consummated – but now on a firmer platform – the platform of reality. Let me ask you a question – how many couples do you know where the husband and the wife are the "same". I can't seem to find even one, from my experience. They are all different – one likes broccoli, the other hates it – one likes traveling, the other doesn't – and the list is infinitely endless.

The moral of the story is very simple. Firstly, we should build our relationship in line with the laws of nature, rather than against it – that is, accept the differences, and promise to create oneness out of diversity. Secondly, appreciate the differences, rather than abhorring them. Differences can be very beautiful. Sameness can breed boredom. And, incidentally, don't we all love variety, and seek variety in every aspect of our life – foods, flowers, tasks, and so on – then why does variety bother us in relationships?

2. Identity and Co-Dependence

Another feeling that can grab you in the first few years after marriage, and can start affecting your relationship is with regard to self-identity and co-dependence. Not too long ago, you were a person with a unique and independent "identity" – the "identity" that you had achieved after so much hard work and perseverance during your Breakfast time. Now, with a feeling of possessiveness – a natural by-product of all good marriages – you feel suffocated – you feel you are losing your identity.

And somehow, you have reached such a mental state, that you now equate "loss of identity" to "loss of independence", or "loss of the self". And the more you think about it, the more you cling to your "me-ness" rut – which, of course, is the opposite of "two-getherness".

Along with the feelings of "loss of identity" comes the feelings of "co-dependence". You are now trying to equate co-dependency with "surrender" – "defeat" – "failure" – "loss of self" – while in my dictionary, they all mean "togetherness". Remember! You virtually took an oath to honour and accept each other's unique identity and independence, and you promised to enhance co-dependence.

Co-dependence, to me, simply means that you are trustfully dependent on the other, on what the other can do best. It means sharing the chores that each one of you can do best. It means trusting your partner, even with your life. Co-dependency is extremely important and a pre-requisite for a good relationship. It gives each of you the feeling, and the satisfaction, that you are useful – that you are wanted – that the other can confidently depend on you. And this feeling is important because it embodies a feeling of trust, and "trust" is the basis of every good relationship. If there is no dependence, it gives a feeling that the other is either egotistic or self-centered.

For me, co-dependency is the most beautiful thing in a marital relationship. It is so comforting – so blissful – to depend on each other – especially when the underlying basis of co-dependency is trust. What a beautiful feeling to know that my wife will adequately look after the house, the children, the social agenda, the grocery shopping – besides her own job. In my case, for example, I can't buy even a loaf of bread right – but that doesn't make me stupid – it's simply that I love and trust my wife to do the needful. If my wife, for example, were not there to look after our social agenda, nobody would, perhaps, ever invite me to a party – that's how socially inept I am, and that's how much trust I have in my co-dependency. And what a feeling of relief my wife has to know that I will look after – paying the bills on time - taking the garbage out – cutting the grass – shovelling the snow – taking kids to the park (perhaps together) – and so on.

Even if you change the roles of these chores, you are still going to do the chores that need to be done, whosoever does them. So how does it matter who does what, they are all just chores. Taking the garbage out is no better or worse than cleaning the floor – they are both meaningless but necessary chores of life and living.

What is even more surprising, or perhaps what bothers me even more is to see so many books, as well as so many professionals and scholars, preaching to people to denounce co-dependency – to fight for independence. If you wanted to be independent – why did you get married in the first place? Why do you want to make your marriage a perpetual battleground in the name of independence or non-co-dependency? I think these professionals are the ones who are the catalysts in breakings of relationships – perhaps that fifty percent divorce rate is because of them. In fact, I think that these professionals are the ones who really need help.

3. The Mental Tape

This concept has been adequately described in chapter 8. The relationship discord is a by-product of the "mental tape" effect. Both partners' mental tape about each other gets filled up with antagonistic feelings over time – until they reach the boiling point – the tape is now full – no more room left – the relationship goes into a spasm – and ultimately to bankruptcy and breakdown.

As indicated earlier, there is an important point to note about the filling of the mental tape. Many a times, in a marital relationship, we take things for granted, and we say things to each other that we think are trivial, harmless, without intentions or just part of the rut and routine of living together – and we carry on with those kinds of silent confrontations over time. But the problem is that you don't know how your partner is taking it. There is a possibility that what is trivial according to you is not so trivial according to the feelings, emotions, and interpretations of your partner. Your partner is not taking these skirmishes in a lighter sense, but he/she is rather construing them as challenges to his/her way of thinking – as naggings – as destructive criticism.

Your partner may not react to these continuous verbal connotations and outbursts as and when they happen, but instead, he/she may be building up bad emotional feelings about these seemingly trivial remarks over time. The result – a whole lifetime of accumulated anger and antagonism, which, one day, may blow up to destroy the relationship. And, the worst part of it is that when it happens – you get completely taken by surprise – you don't know why it has happened – you were never aware of the building of this mental antagonism – you always thought of these as innocent gestures. Really and truly, you only come to know of this tape's existence when your partner starts replaying the tape – incident by incident – and starts opening up the dead graves of discontent and anger. And if you are still truly honest, you may be saying: I wish I had known earlier about this tape – I wish I had been given a chance so that I could have rectified and corrected the antagonism right when it took birth.

So the moral of the story is that it is important in a marital relationship to see to it that you are sensitive and compassionate to each other's feelings and emotions – that you don't degrade and dehumanize each other's point of view pursuant to what you think is right, or as per your own self-assumptions of right and wrong. Never underestimate the power of simple, innocent, and honest day-to-day verbal confrontations and interactions – their cumulative effect can be very strong and devastating – it can yield enormous damage to the health of your relationship – and you may not even be aware of it.

4. Change of Perspective

If marriage is "Marketing" – relationship is "Strategy". At the start of the process of marriage, your total concentration is on how to find the right mate and how to consummate the relationship. That is quite a difficult task indeed, yet you found the right person and you established the relationship – bravo – congratulations. Wait a minute – let me give you the bad news: if you think getting married was a difficult task and a great achievement, wait until you lead the married life – the maintenance of a marital relationship is even more difficult.

Since at the time of marriage, you are totally busy in consummating the relationship, you never think or plan for how the relationship will be carried on. Very soon, just after a few years of marriage – when the honeymoon is over and reality starts dawning – changes start coming into your married life. And these are changes for which you were never prepared at the time of marriage, and these are the changes that are now beginning to erode the happiness and harmony of your relationship. Many changes come over time in any marriage – they are a normal part of life and living – but how you are prepared for those changes, and how you handle and balance out those changes determines how your relationship will grow and progress. Here are some important facets of married life that call for understanding, planning, and balanced thinking:

- You started the relationship with just the two of you, and perhaps, at the time of marriage, you did not think that the relationship circle would expand any farther than either the two of you, or up to your children. That was the first strategic mistake. As life moves forward, more people come into the domain of relationships – for example, all the relatives that both of you inherited by virtue of your consummation. Now what's happening? Your own relationship is fine and happy, but it is being badly badgered by the intervention of your relatives. And this is causing continual stress and antagonism between you two, and the daily skirmishes are taking your relationship towards bankruptcy and breakdown. You have to learn how to balance out those aspects maturely, or more importantly – you should have planned the resolution strategy for such a happening far in advance of its inception because they are a normal part of any relationship, and they are bound to come into play in any relationship.

- Next, your individual busyness with your own separate routines is taking you apart – you are being absorbed in your own separate busy routines of life – and you are drifting apart. You are getting edgy about it because you think it is eroding your togetherness. This is a wrong way of looking at things. The chores of life, as you know, are a necessary part of life – they have to happen for life and living. You have to understand that you have to keep the priorities of life and the togetherness of your relationship as two distinctly separate entities. You have to balance out your life – and once you do that, the chores and the togetherness would both happen automatically as two non-conflicting parallel streams of life – there won't be any conflict – you will accomplish all the chores and tasks and still feel as together with each other as you did at the time of your marriage vows.

5. Ego-Sensitivity versus Feelings-Sensitivity

We know that men and women are dramatically different in their behavior and attitude – but, what about the difference in their sensitivities – how does that influence the relationship? That is what I want to examine vis-à-vis my new premise. I shall elucidate my point by putting forth the following two new conjectures.

- Men are ego-sensitive
- Women are feelings-sensitive

Before I begin, I must say that I am speaking in terms of observational generalities – that is to say, when I refer to men as ego-sensitive and women as feelings- sensitive, I don't mean to say that that is the status quo. Because the reverse can be equally true as well – that is, men have feelings too, and women have egos as well.

The differences in sensitivities have a profound effect on the way we behave and act, and hence on our relationships – and, therefore, it's understanding would provide us with more information to resolve our relationship dilemma. My aim is to highlight the characteristics of ego-sensitivity and feelings-sensitivity, and indicate how each spouse can utilize this information to mould and manoeuvre their relationship towards better harmony.

Ego-Sensitivity

Let's begin with men first. To men, ego is the most precious possession – whether consciously or unconsciously. To some extent, men and ego are synonyms – they are two sides of the same coin. Men can virtually do anything to uphold their ego. They would never let their ego face insult, defeat, or surrender. Their ego-sensitivity is so high that a single syllable spoken wrongly or misinterpreted can tilt their emotional balance and send them into an antagonistic spasm, and they would be ready and armed to fight back to safeguard their ego. And this is simply because men tend to associate their ego with self-esteem, self-respect, self-integrity, and self-pride – in fact, with the whole of their self-existence.

Unfortunately, most of us have no control over our ego – rather, our ego controls and dictates our lives. To put it in a metaphorical manner, it is not that we won't let our ego get hurt – it is that our ego won't let us get our ego hurt. When a man's ego gets hurt – rightly or falsely – his anger and aggressiveness also comes to the forefront – and in that mode, his maturity suffers a setback, and consequently, his behavior becomes unworthy of what he actually is.

When compared to women, this, I think, is an inherent weakness of men's personality, and this is the root cause of many unhappy relationships. But whatever the case, men's ego-sensitivity is a fact of life, and it has to be handled sensitively. And for the sake of maintaining relationship harmony, women have a very significant role to play in this scenario. In doing so, the first thing a woman has to know is that she cannot afford to hurt the man's sensitive ego. In what ways can she hurt her man's ego, and what can she do to avoid it? Here are some possible indicators to tell you that you can hurt his ego:

- If you directly challenge his "kingship" without adequate reason or explanation.
- If you nag him constantly and make him feel that he is 100% wrong 100% of the time – that he is good for nothing – and that you are right 100% of the time, which really comes to your putting a zero-tolerance on his being right.
- If you insult him and put him down in the presence of others. And, of course, this one is a complete no-no.

With this argument, it's possible that some women would say: Why do I have to tolerate this – why do I have to bend backwards. But if you look at the scenario in a positive and calm manner, you would see that it is really not bending backwards or giving in, it's a matter of maturity of understanding to save a relationship. There are two ways of looking at this incongruity:

- The first way is to strike back and say: why do I have to worry about his ego – I have an ego too – what about my ego? In this situation, you are making the same mistake as the man – you are letting your pride block your better judgment – tit for tat is totally damaging to the relationship.
- The second and more intelligent way is to hold your horses – be patient and humble, because your spouse needs your help. After all, you love him, and who better is there than you to give him help – and, of course, you do also have a desire to maintain the relationship harmony. Remember! Making yourself humble does not, in any way, mean defeat or insult or surrender, it is simply a matter of your maturity and compassion to help the person you love. Anger can never heal anger, it rather further aggravates it. Only kindness can defeat anger, and kindness is almost second nature to women in the relationship.

And even if, as a woman, you want to look at this whole issue from the perspective of winning and losing, you will be the one who is always winning, because with your mature and patient womanly mindset, you can get almost anything done from the man, just as long as you don't hurt his ego, but instead, make him feel that he is the "king", even when he is not.

From this humble method of relationship interplay, I would like to identify a specific scenario that applies to overly aggressive women who continually badger and nag their husbands. If you continually hurt his ego-sensitivity with your aggressiveness and immature feeling-sensitivity – then you run the following risks:

- He will continually fight back, and life will become an unending battleground.
- He may do what you want him to do, without a fight – but he may withdraw from you emotionally, and go into silent separations, which is even worse – because withdrawal might make him weak and aloof. And if that happens, you may start to complain that your husband is less than a manly man – that he doesn't behave like a man – like other men do – but then of course, that would be very silly on your part because you are forgetting that you are the one who has made him like that anyway.

I have an interesting recipe for you ladies – to achieve your goal – the goal of whatever you want to get done from your husband. I annotate this recipe as "reverse psychology", and I would take a meaninglessly simple example to elucidate my theory. This idea is already identified in chapter 28.

Let's begin with a scenario: you would like your husband to take the garbage out when he comes home from work. So your goal is:" to get the garbage out" – and remember that I emphasized that you must have a clearly defined goal. The husband comes home, picks up his beer, and sits down on the sofa to relax. But you want to get the garbage out – now now. You have two ways to handle this situation:

- One, to shout at him and ask him to take the garbage out right away, rather than sipping his beer and being a couch potato. By this method – you may achieve your goal – but it may leave some internal scars of anger in him.
- The other way – the way that I am suggesting – is to say to him: honey! I am sure, you must be exhausted from work – why don't you relax with your drink and I would take the garbage out.

And I can tell you with utmost certainty, that he will throw away everything, and jump up from his sofa, and take the garbage out "first". That is what I call — "reverse psychology". So here is the analysis: you had a goal — your goal is achieved without a fight — then why achieve it with a fight — why arm your ego and his ego — why create anger and hostility of feelings and emotions for no reason whatsoever.

Feelings-Sensitivity

Let's turn our attention to women now. While women are better able to control their ego-sensitivity than men, they are more vulnerable to problems associated with feelings-sensitivity. Women are generally feelings-sensitive — their world revolves around the satisfaction of their feeling-oriented desires. For example, they want their husband to care for them, love them, touch them, take them out for dinners, bring flowers for them, etc.

Women are more prone to, sort of, showy things — more subtle, but diplomatic. For example, they need to be actually told that you love them. As a man, it may be hard for you to do that, because you are not feelings-sensitive. Also because you love your wife inside your heart anyway. But that's not enough for the wife — you have to show it by saying it in order to please her feelings-sensitivity. Women are generally easy to please, and I mean that in the good sense. They are happy in little things. So as a man, you have to do those little things. Little things may be trivial or meaningless for you, but they are important for those feelings-sensitive species — you have got to do them — you have got to show off. The simple rule for men, therefore, is: never do anything that hurts her feelings and emotions — for if you do, she will never ever forget it, nor would ever forgive you for that — at least, internally in her mind. She can keep those hurt-feelings permanently in her mental-tape. Whether it is a weakness of personality, or whatever it is, this is where women are more egotistic than men — not forgetting — not forgiving — at least those acts that hurt their feelings and emotions.

A few observations about "hurt" — whether it is an ego-hurt (men) or a feelings-hurt (women):

- A hurt can cause a scar that may never go away — despite all cosmetic surgery.
- Trust and feelings are like a thin thread — once broken — you can tie a knot — but there will always be a knot.

- Feelings are like a mirror – once a crack comes by way of hurting or betraying the trust – that crack will never be filled.

So here is the moral of the story:

- Be sensitive to each other's sensitivities.
- Don't walk over on each other just to prove a point – or just to get even – or just to get the feeling of victory, because that victory is a false victory, and would be very costly for your relationship.
- Never ever insult each other in front of others. Also never discuss or argue your differences in front of others – do it alone with each other.
- Respect each other's space – mental and physical.
- Respect each other's point of view.

6. Love

Finally, a few words on "love". No, I am not going to write another manual on love – there are already too many written on the subject, yet I have a very unique thought about love and relationships that I wish to discuss.

A time comes in the married life when we start drifting away from each other – the distance increases – the mental tape is full of angry feelings. A funny thing happens – instead of reconciling and seeking each other's company – we begin the outward journey of seeking the company and love (only platonic) of our own type (sex), rather than the opposite sex – that is to say – women become more engrossed in the company of women – their friends, sisters, mother, cousins, etc. – and men get more engrossed with the company of men. And sometimes, their love and care for this new group, of their own kind, can even exceed the love and care they give or are supposed to give to each other – as husband and wife.

To some extent – it's a normal behavior – there is nothing wrong or bad about it. But, in some cases, the gap between a husband and wife and the transference of love to your own sex-type can reach such a stage that an unseen, unspoken, and silent repulsion sets in between the couple, and they start preferring their own sexes more than the other sex. Slowly, the distance between them increases – even a simple touch to each other's body becomes a rare event, because a kind of other-sex-repulsion effect sets in.

This repulsion-effect is circular in nature – it happens because you drift apart in your relationship due to some relationship discord or bad feelings, and you drift apart because you have transferred your love onto your own sex-type. This type of problem is, typically, more prevalent with women than with men. Because transference of love between men is not so common – they simply transfer friendship. Men, in general, love the other sex – women – more than their own sex-type anyway, because they are always looking for love and fulfillment from a feelings-sensitive person – the woman, rather than from another ego-sensitive person – the man.

Women, on the other hand, manifest a feeling – especially in the Dinner Phase – as if they have had enough of the ego-sensitive person – the man. These women want to revert back to their roots – to their own type – the feelings-sensitive type – the woman. So they tend to seek the company of women more than the company of their own men – at times far more than what is naturally healthy. For these women, man is just a required part of the overall picture, not a desired part of the picture – man is an unavoidable necessity. These women do not have a feeling-feeling for the man; they have necessity-feeling for the spouse.

For a happy and healthy marriage, the first and foremost requirement is for each spouse to love the other – the woman should have a genuine desire and a sense of feel, touch, and love for the masculine sex – the husband, and the husband should have a desire for the other sex – the feminine – the wife.

In the Dinner Phase, many a women get more and more busy in their own worlds, or in the worlds of their own kind – more than the world of their husbands. They may be busy in their spas, girl-nights, fitness programs, or they may tend to spend more time with ladies or their own female relatives. There is nothing wrong with this as long as it doesn't override the threshold of their togetherness with their own man. If it goes overboard, it will bring in "lonesome-togetherness" or "silent separations".

There is nothing more beautiful than "alive-togetherness", and there is nothing more devastating than "dead-togetherness". And incidentally, it's all in the head – a relationship between a husband and wife is a matter of the mind, heart, and soul – and not only of the body.

21

THE DILEMMA

"Love is – when a little girl, whose father has died – says:
Daddy! Come back to hold my hand just once more."

We have almost come to the end of our journey in understanding the nature of our relationships, and we have taken all the necessary and requisite steps to ensure the continuity of a happy and harmonious relationship. The awakening process signifies our commitment and testifies to the fact that:

- We are sensitive to each other's feelings and emotions.
- We are respectful of each other's self-esteem, identity, and opinions.
- We are humble to each other, and we love and honour togetherness

Can anything go wrong now – I am afraid "yes". Things can still go wrong – and this is the dilemma – the warning – that I want to bring to your attention so that you would be aware of it and be able to handle it adequately, should the dilemma happen. The dilemma is with regard to your "ego", which can still jump in to spoil everything – even despite the fact that you have worked hard to control your ego to better your relationship. How can that happen?

Suppose, for a minute, that you have done everything with utmost honesty and tenacity that was needed to be done to harmonize your relationship. You have humbled yourself down – you respect your partner's opinion and individuality – you love your spouse and you constantly endeavour towards achieving relationship harmony and happiness – and so on. In fact, you have reached a stage where you have humbled yourself down so much that even if, for example, the other person hits you on your left cheek, you are ready to offer the right cheek if the person wants to hit you again – that is – you have sacrificed your ego for the sake of relationship harmony. And also, your conceptual framework has reached a stage where you believe that if you humble yourself down to that extent, the other person would also become mellow and modest and would never hit you again — and perhaps would even feel ashamed of hitting you in the first place.

Suddenly your perception takes a direct hit because the other person keeps hitting you — despite your humble surrenders. By the way — you understand that my reference to "hitting" doesn't mean verbatim physical hit — it's only a connotation — it means relationship dissension and fighting. Suddenly you get a rude awakening — your dreams of wanting to become a better person seem to get shattered — your sleeping ego, which you had worked hard to tame, has suddenly awakened with a bad hurt. The situation is now forcing you to reconsider your stance of niceness. Perhaps you want to throw away your niceness and humbleness, you want to fight back — to revert back to your old self — back to what you were before you started on your new journey of self-awakenings, inner-evolution, and personal enhancement. Thoughts swirl around in your mind, and you say to yourself: I did what was needed to be done to ameliorate the relationship — I did my part as nicely as I possibly could do — what do I get in return — insults and more insults. What's the use of changing me — myself — when the other person is never going to change?

Your sleeping giant — your ego — rises to the occasion. You begin to stir up the harmony of your relationship all over again: why should I be the one who has to bend backwards all the time — why should I be the one who should change — why not him — I haven't done anything bad any more or any less than him — if I am at fault, he is at fault too — it's mutual — we have to be equally responsible — it has to be two-sided, not one-sided. I have changed myself for the sake of relationship harmony, but he doesn't want to change — he will never change. Hell with it — it's not going to work — I am not going to bend backwards anymore — I hate him — I am going to hate him until I die — I will never forgive him.

That's the "dilemma".

The dilemma is that, your assumption — and a right assumption of course, that both parties have to work equally hard to ameliorate the relationship — has not been effectively realized, and your ego has received a direct hit. You are feeling that you have been humiliated — you sense a feeling of defeat — that you have made a fool of yourself — and consequently, the forces of evil are once again taking control of you and throwing you back into the same morbid chasm of bad relationships that you were originally in – and from which it took you so long to come out.

Heart and hurt have a very close relationship, and you are surely hurt. This one-sided reconciliation effort is raising questions in your mind: who is to decide who is right or who is wrong in a relationship discord – why him – why not me. So this is the dilemma I wanted to forewarn you about – that all through your process of reconciliation – remedying and rejuvenating your relationship, you can face these types of feelings, almost at every step of the way – the dilemma – "why me, why not him".

How you handle it is going to be totally up to you. All I can say is that a relationship is a matter of mutual love and understanding – don't let a single setback destroy your patience and determination. Dilemmas like these are generally a phantom of your thinking – if they appear, they will also disappear. Just hold your horses – don't rush into personifying the dilemma as a setback – for, after all, we are talking about the person you love – and surely, love is far stronger than a simple setback. You need to maintain your sense of stability, maturity, patience, and determination to move forward to your chosen path.

SECTION 5
FINAL FRONTIERS
THE RESOLVE

22
BREAK THE SILENCE

"A beautiful relationship is a matter of the soul;
It's never born – it never dies."

With this chapter, we now enter the zone of final frontiers – the zone of the resolution of the problem, once and for all. And I must first discuss the most fundamental problem that affects the whole relationship domain – the problem of "silence" – the problem of lack of communication.

The problem of "silence" is a generic one, but it is also a very high-impact problem – and if and when it happens in a relationship, it blocks all roads to the recovery of relationship harmony. It is, therefore, of utmost importance that I discuss this problem before embarking upon my journey to outline solutions and guidelines to achieving relationship harmony. For without the understanding of how "silence" affects the free flow of communication – most essential for conflict resolution – no solution can really be effective. My suggestions and guidelines will be generic in nature, yet they would be applicable to any relationship scenario.

Whenever a relationship goes bad, the first calamity is "communication". A sheet of silence spreads over the relationship landscape. We go quietly into our own worlds – into silent separations. We do carry on with the normal day-to-day chores of life and relationships, but we give each other the "royal silent treatment". We don't speak to each other for days, or don't speak as happily or as frequently as we normally do when the relationship is okay. We also don't confront each other aggressively, just so that the relationship won't lead to breakings, because for one reason or another, we want to maintain the relationship, howsoever painful it may be living in it.

Why does the silence occur? Silence is an outcome of hurt feelings. When we get hurt by our partner's attitude, a sense of anger sets in, and the first outcome of that anger is "silence". Why can't we break the silence? Because our false ego-pride won't let us do it – because, for the ego, it's a sign of defeat – and that's a no-no for the ego?

The dilemma is how to break the silence, because without it, we can never reconcile the fractured relationship. And the more we stay in silence, the more anger and antagonism we will accumulate inside of us, and the longer it will take to reconcile. In fact, "silence" is the single most important and intractable entity in the relationship domain that impedes the smooth flow of relationship harmony. And unless you can break the cycle of silence, you cannot expect to connect with the other person in order to open up and start the harmonization process. The basic dilemma, therefore, is:

- How to break the silence?
- How to begin to communicate with each other?
- How to start the process of reconciliation?

In light of the above discussion, here, then, are a few simple thoughts for this very common, but complex, problem:

- Firstly, as indicated in an earlier chapter also, you should draw up a list, mentally or physically, of all the issues for which you are angry with each other.
- Compartmentalize this list into three segments: minor issues, normal issues, and serious issues.
- Since the aim is to break the silence, pick up one minor issue out of the list as a starting point. Remember! Don't pick up a serious issue first – nor try to pick up too many issues together – or you will further aggravate the situation.
- Find a suitable time and place to open up the discussion on that one minor issue.
- Make sure that your opening presentation does not signal putting blame on the other. Rather, play the game through what is known as "Reverse Psychology" – a method that I have elaborated before – by bringing the blame, for the moment at least, upon your own self. Of course, this requires a definite agreement with your prideful ego, who may not let you do so.
- This approach will help you to break the ice – the silence barrier – and that's the window of opportunity you were looking for.
- Reconcile with each other as amicably as possible – so that both parties feel comfortable, happy, unhurt, and "winners".

- Once the silence is broken, your doors to harmonization are wide open, and you can now carry on with the reconciliation process for all other outstanding issues, but indeed, one issue at a time, and also at appropriate moments of time and place. Like this, you can go from minor to major issues slowly and systematically, and achieve total reconciliation and total relationship harmony.

23
EMPTY THE TAPE

"True love is without condition."

In chapter 8, I introduced my new concept of the "mental-tape effect". As I propounded, a mental-tape is a blatant reality and we all have it – a tape for each of the people we know. And this tape is a storehouse of our impressions about the other person "as we see it" – the way we feel about the other person. Unfortunately, it is not how the other person actually may or may not be; it is simply a collection of our own interpretations of what we think about the other. For that matter, the fact is that the mere existence of the tape is harmful to our relationships, because we always tend to interact with the other person, only through our impressions on the tape, and not independently of the tape. We do not give the relationship a fair and equitable chance to grow and flourish, because our preconceived hang-ups and emotional constraints about the others impede the normal flow of harmony between us.

So as you can see, in order to have permanent relationship happiness, you have to make an effort to correct this deficiency – to amend the tape, or better yet, to destroy the tape altogether. You must understand and come to terms with the fact that you created the tape and therefore, you are the only one responsible for its elimination, and you are the only one who can do it. But I can guarantee you that you can do it, should you desire, but it would, of course, only happen when you put your heart and soul into it. Let me begin with two basic guidelines:

- If possible, try to get into the habit of not creating the tape in the first place. Deal with each person or each situation as it occurs – only on its face value, without bringing in the past – the tape effect.
- If you must create the tape, then keep emptying it as frequently as you fill it – don't hoard and accumulate feelings and impressions.

Let me now give you some suggestions on how to deal with the tape effect, and how to empty or amend the tape. Because you have thousands of tapes in your head (memory), one for each of the people you know, and you can't amend them all at once, I will outline the basic framework of the overall process that you can utilize to empty the tapes one by one, or as you confront the relationship situations. And for the sake of brevity and hands-on understanding, we shall begin the explanation of the process by taking the example of the most important tape you have – that for your spouse:

- Every so often, sit down quietly and peacefully in a comfortable place – alone, just by yourself.
- Now, replay the tape and see what is on it – what kinds of feelings, grudges, or impressions you are holding for your spouse on the tape.
- Identify the sore issues.
- Evaluate, as judiciously as possible, the seriousness and intensity of these sore points. Rank them in order of their seriousness.
- Study carefully the rights and the wrongs, and see whether they emanate from what your spouse said or did, or have arisen from your own interpretation of what your spouse said or did.
- Consider, for each sore point, the possibility that your spouse is not wrong – that you can be wrong also.
- Now prepare yourself – mentally and consciously – to begin the process of emptying the tape.
- Firstly, confine yourself to emptying whatever you can by your own mental efforts. Look, first, for the "not-so-serious" points of dissension – evaluate their worth – see if they are really worthy of being kept on the tape, even against the health of your relationship. Try to drop those issues one by one and rid the tape of those unwanted trivial issues that hamper the smooth flow of your relationship happiness.
- Next, pick up the serious issues, or issues that you think are serious. Take one issue at a time, because if you take all of them together, you will create an emotional jam, and nothing will be accomplished.
- Evaluate the one issue that you have chosen, and see its rights and wrongs. Assess, as honestly as you can, whether your spouse is wrong or you yourself are wrong.

- Now, bring in what I call "humble surrenders" — the power of humbleness — to accept the fact that you can be wrong also — to give your spouse the respect he/she deserves for being right.
- Now try to find a suitable time and place to discuss the issue with your spouse. Be open-minded. Don't start the process by blaming your spouse. Make it a genuine attempt to find the rights and the wrongs — rather than finding faults and blaming each other. Find a mutually agreeable solution.
- Continue this process until you have rid yourself of the unwanted baggage you are carrying — the mental tape. Clear the tape altogether and try to fill it with good feelings of love and affection for your spouse.

The key to this process of emptying the tape is through a continuous dialogue with the other person. And the ingredients of the process are: open-mindedness, humble surrenders, willingness to humble down your ego, strength to accept your own faults, a keen desire to amend yourself, and finally, a passionate desire to create harmony and happiness in your relationships.

24
CONTROL THE RIGHTEOUSNESS SYNDROME

"External wealth cannot eliminate internal poverty."

In chapters 9 and 10, I introduced two very important behavioral factors – "Variety" and "Righteousness-Arrogance" – that exert enormous influence on our behavior. Now in this chapter, I shall present some general guidelines on how to control and channel those personality traits to our advantage. By now, I am assuming that you have a good appreciation and understanding of the power of these two factors – GG1 (Variety) and GG2 (Righteousness), or maybe their unseen and un-admitted power over our relationships. Let us recapitulate the underlying precept of these factors:

- Variety (GG1): That every person is different – has a different thinking mind – has different likings and dislikings – would behave and act differently – and has the right to do so.
- Righteousness (GG2): The "Omni-Supreme" syndrome: Thinking that we know all – that what we know is always right – that we are the smartest of all – and that all must follow us.

In the previous discussion, I also annotated these two as God's gift to humanity. Maybe we have to de-annotate them for the moment and consider them as man-made so that we can try making some changes in them that will facilitate a smooth and palatable flow of relationship happiness. To begin with, I would like to do a reality check and outline some basic suggestions:

- Firstly, you have to come to terms with yourself and understand that every person is different – and there is nothing wrong or bad about it – it's just that we are all different and we should accept and enjoy the variety. Doesn't it sound funny that on one hand we love variety in almost every aspect of our life and living – and on the other, we cannot tolerate variety in our

behavior and attitude. We don't want to accept differences in
our thinking, in our likes and dislikes, and in our actions.

- Next, you have to continuously remind yourself that you are
not the only one who knows all and is always right – that others
are as smart as you are, if not smarter.

- Try considering the situation in this way – that if you think
that others are different, and therefore wrong – and that others
don't know as much as you do – then how would you feel if
others thought the same about you. And if that makes you feel
bad, then think of how bad the others must be feeling about
your behavior towards them. Which means that life is a two-
way street – that you will reap what you sow – that you will be
behaved with by the others exactly the same way you behave
with them.

- Finally, a blatant reality – how can your relationship function if
you always confront each other with an uncompromising ego?
How can two negatives survive and function in a relationship
milieu? If you have any desire or hope, to any degree, of creating
permanent harmony in your relationships, you will have to bend
backwards – to accept and respect each other's individuality
and different points of view – to compromise and look for a
middle ground – and that is the ultimate recipe for happiness.

The solution to this enigma lies in bringing a change in your
thinking and attitude, and each person has to undergo this change by
himself/herself. The change has to be brought in you by you – and the
most important tool for that is "introspective thinking and analysis". It
is through this inner thinking that you will realize that you do have the
tendency to behave like this – and this first step of "acceptance" holds
the key to moving forward in the amendment process. And with a strong
desire to make amends, you will be on your way to recovery. Here then,
are a few guidelines:

- Every so often, go for a long walk, alone – or sit in a quite
and comfortable room. Talk to yourself, openly and freely. Ask
yourself: why don't you accept different points of view – why
are you so egotistic and arrogant. Now, answer these questions
frankly and honestly – because nobody else is listening – you
are all alone. Surely, you can tell your self the truth – for if you

are not honest with your own self – how can you be expected to be honest with others? "The highest form of accountability is always to the self." "The highest form of disgrace comes when you have fallen in your own eyes."

- Repeat the same exercise during your social gatherings. Quietly observe your self – your behavior – and see if you are suffering from this disease of arrogance and righteousness – see if you constantly negate people's opinions because they are different from yours. See if you have the tendency to think that you know all, that you are always right, and that others are wrong.

- Now, the acceptance mode – to come to terms with yourself, to accept your weaknesses. Unless you accept your shortcomings, you have nothing to amend.

- Next, you go into the analysis mode – to ask yourself the questions: why are you the way you are – why do you think and behave like this – what internal feelings, emotions, or internal chemistry forces you to think like that. Try to find answers as to why you do what you do – item-by-item – question-by-question. Get some real, concrete, and workable answers from your own self.

- The final step involves going into the Nirvanic zone (Nirvana: state of blessedness achieved by the extinction of the self) – where you take control of things to make sure that your ego doesn't control your thinking, and to reduce or eliminate your internal anger and antagonism. Appreciate diversity, respect individuality, and avoid complacency and arrogance.

25
DROP THE EGO

*"You can achieve happiness,
As soon as you can define it."*

In chapter 11, we elaborated on the most elusive and the most ambiguous of all personality traits – the "Ego". As indicated earlier: we really don't know what ego is – whether it exists or not – or if it does, where it resides in our body. Yet mysteriously, at the same time – somehow we know that there is certainly something that resides inside us and profoundly affects and dictates our attitude and behavior, mostly in the damaging and negative manner – and we generally call it the "ego".

Notwithstanding its elusiveness though, what we do know is that the main function of ego is to defend and safeguard our self-esteem and false pride. For example, when we brag about our superiority, generally a misrepresentation of actuality – or when other people challenge and attack our convictions, mostly faulty and prideful convictions – we seek the ego's help to fight for us, to defend and safeguard our self-esteem. In fact, our ego is always there ready and prepared to uphold and safeguard our faults and idiosyncrasies.

Examining the role of ego, it is not difficult to infer that our own ego forces us to misrepresent us. It encourages us to present distorted manifestations of our abilities. Under the influence of ego:

- We would like to portray our abilities as more than they actually are.
- We would have the tendency to misrepresent our capabilities.
- We would like to portray our abilities with pride and arrogance.

And on top of it, we would like our ego to strongly uphold our wrong convictions and defend our self-esteem. So as you can see, despite all of our understanding of the issue, we have a problem – an intractable problem of gigantic proportions – "what to do with this ambiguous entity – the ego". How do we control and channel this negative ego-energy towards positive directions? The problem is further compounded by the fact that, despite our understanding that ego is our own worst enemy, we still seem to love it – and we feel proud of it.

After considerable thought and contemplation, I was able to come up with a simple model for the functioning of the ego, as appended in chapter 11, which provided me with a clear vision of how to tame and channel this ego-energy to our advantage. As indicated in chapter 11, ego has two functional modes: active mode (waking state), and passive mode (resting or sleeping state). In the active mode, it is too difficult to communicate with the ego – you cannot argue with ego – it is ready to fight back at a moment's notice, even when a fight is not warranted – and even when the confrontation is for a wrong cause. But in the passive mode (which I annotate as the "dropped ego" mode), the ego is in the humbled-down mood and is more receptive to a more realistic stance. This gave me an idea: to find out its resting spots and find out what we can do to make the ego stay longer and more often in those passive modes – because these are the states in which the ego is least harmful.

So, with this basic premise, I would now introduce my new paradigms for controlling the ego-energy. Basically, our aim is to:

- Make sure that we don't, unnecessarily, aggravate the devil – the ego.
- Make sure that we don't awaken the giant.
- Make sure that we keep the ego dropped in the passive state, for as long as possible, and as often as we can.

Let me now present some fresh new ideas that I have developed to overcome and alleviate the unwanted interference by the ego into our behavioral attitude, so as to afford us the opportunity to improve the happiness of our relationships.

Humble Surrenders

This involves humbling down your ego-arrogance and exercising mutual respect so as to live into the relationship at par with each other's self-esteem. To understand the need for humble surrenders, you should try to visualize how your ego-arrogance impacts your interactions.

Think of it this way – if you have a large arrogant ego, others have it too – as large or, perhaps, larger than yours. If your behavior is arrogant and uncompromising, so can be that of others as well. If you want to impose your ego's will onto others, how are others going to tolerate it and let you do that? Why should anybody keep a relationship with you at all under those circumstances? And as a final nail in the coffin – how would you feel if others behave with you as badly and egotistically as you do with them? Would you like to keep and maintain a relationship with them under these conditions?

How can relationships survive and function at all when both parties maintain and uphold their uncompromising ego-arrogance and their own convictions? Somewhere somebody has to bend backwards to allow the relationship some breathing room – to grow and flourish. And that is where humble surrenders come into play. Humble surrenders is not what the name might suggest – a surrender – defeat – let-down – or insult to the ego or self-esteem. Humble surrender is simply a matter of extending a hand in friendship and love in order to create and sustain a cordial relationship. It is a mode of living at par with each other's convictions and self-respect.

Split-Second-Silence

Another amelioration technique – this new concept is about "reacting" to the humble side of the other person. Whenever somebody – your spouse, for example – says something derogatory to you –don't react and respond instantaneously – give a conscious split-second pause before you respond. This pause will give your mind the chance to re-reflect on the situation, and your response will be more subtle, mature, and appropriate. It is an excellent technique for all interactive situations, for it creates a momentary vacuum in which the ego is dormant and does not override your maturity level. Consequently, the ensuing action, being the result of pure wisdom, have a greater chance of being accepted and being right.

Freeze-Frame the Moment

This relates to the concept of "Mindfulness" – a state of mind when you are aware of the present moment only – not the past – not the future. Your concentration is single-focused, and your energies are directed only to the present – the task at hand – which, indeed, allows you to derive the greatest pleasure from whatever you are doing. These moments are ego-less domains – for the ego is absent or passive in these moments. Ego doesn't recognize the present, for the ego is only either the actual past or the imaginary future. In these moments, ego is dropped – there is nobody to fight with you. The idea is to "freeze-Frame" these moments. Your wisdom and maturity is, then, at its best, because there is no ego-interference. Once you have experienced one such moment, then you go to the next step, which involves getting into the habit of consciously creating such moments – and this would then put the power back in your hands to control your ego the way you deem fit, rather than the ego controlling your behavior, as normally is the case.

A small digression: let me give you a simple exercise for generating a state of "mindfulness":

- Sit on a chair, in a comfortable position.
- Close your eyes.
- Empty your mind of external thoughts.
- Direct your eyes and mind inwards.
- Focus your attention only on the sounds and vibrations of your life-energy, your breath – coming in – going out.
- Concentrate on that until your mind feels nothing else but that life-energy.

A five-minute run of this exercise would make your mind serene and relaxed, and would enhance your mental concentration and state of mindfulness.

Drop the Ego

The basic framework of the concept of "drop the ego" was laid down in chapter 11. The whole idea is to drop the ego in the passive state and keep it there for as long as possible, because in that state, ego is humbled down and does not aggressively interfere with your thought processes. The question to ask is: are there passive states that exist – does ego ever leave the active-waking states to go into resting-sleeping state? Here are some scenarios of the ego's passive states:

- You are lying on a sandy beach – simmering in the sum – watching the waves – you are totally at peace – there is no ego – the phantom is sleeping. Beware! In the split of that second – while still lying in the sand – you now start to think about an unhappy incident that happened back in the office or the fight you had with your spouse – voila! your ego is back again – the phantom is up – to make you restless and irritable. You are tense – even when the beach and the water are still as calm as before.

- You are making love to your spouse – you are both happy and compassionate – there is no ego – the ego is dropped. Beware! Suddenly, you start talking about his mother, or her sister, or about children, or about finances – aggravation sets in and the ego comes alive again – you are both frozen – you can't even make love anymore.

- You are eating your favourite food – you are really enjoying it – you are totally absorbed in the culinary delight – you are single-focused – there is no ego – ego is dropped. Beware! Suddenly, your spouse makes a comment about something – a derogatory comment – and you don't like it – you get angry – voila! – your ego is back again – you can't even swallow the bite you have in your mouth – much less eating more.

Why does the ego not wake up in these situations – like eating, making love, etc. – it is because our entire concentration is single-focused – our energies are directed only to the task at hand – we are not interfering with the sleep of the ego – and the sleeping ego is not interfering with our single-focused task at hand.

What do these scenarios tell us – that it is possible to drop the ego and control it – or put another way – the ego is controllable – the ego is droppable, and therefore, the relationship is open to reconciliations? So then, the simple recipe is: stay in the moment in every and all relationship interactions – never bring the past into the present – that is, the mental-tape of built-up anger of the past.

If you can get into the habit of imitating and generating these states – naturally or artificially in all your relationship interactions – you can avoid ego's unwanted interference – and carry on a happy relationship forever.

26
TAME THE AGGRESSIVENESS

"Victory over the "self" is the greatest of all triumphs."

While discussing the subject of "aggressiveness" in chapter 12, we encountered a difficult question: how do we tame and harness our aggressiveness? And the answer was that there is no magic formula. However, the good news was that aggressiveness is a characteristic that does lend itself to control and, therefore, if we make a concerted effort, we can tame our aggressiveness. There are three steps to the process:

- Realization: A realization of your aggressiveness
- Acceptance: An acceptance of the fact that your behavior is aggressive
- Desire: A desire to harness your aggressiveness

Realization

You cannot, indeed, think of controlling something that you don't even know that you have. It's a common understanding that many aggressive people don't even themselves know that they have an aggressive attitude. However, there are a few simple methods with which this difficulty can be overcome: first, you ask somebody else – somebody close to you – to tell you whether you are aggressive or not; second, you learn from your own observations of your own behavior in different situations.

Let's start with the first method – the best person you can start with is your own spouse, for she is the only person who can tell you the right thing in all honesty. The only thing that you have to take care of is to make sure that she is not afraid of telling you the truth – for fear of making you angry or spoiling the relationship. So you really have to show her your genuine desire to learn about your behavior.

The next method of assessment is by your own self – by observing your own behavior, especially during group conversations and interactions. Carefully notice:

- If you are dominating the conversation – speaking too much.
- If you keep interrupting others when they are talking.
- If your bodily gestures or the tone of your speech impart the feelings of egotism, pushiness, aggressiveness, restlessness, arrogance, and immaturity.

Acceptance

After realization, the next important, but difficult, step is that of acceptance of the fact that your behavior is dominating and pushy in nature. My research indicates that there are very few aggressive people who would ever come straight out and accept that they have a dominating disposition. And I'm sure you must also have encountered many such situations in your own circle of relationships. Then there are people who know well that they are pushy, and of them, some may even announce that fact loudly, because they associate aggressiveness with power, authority, and superiority – and these feelings are, or can be, a means to elevate and embellish their ego's false pride.

Notwithstanding however, if you have any desire to harness your negative aggressive energy to a positive and mature state of mind, you have no choice but to first accept your current state of pushiness, and then prepare yourself for the final step – to know how to control and harness your aggressiveness.

Harnessing

The process of taming your aggressiveness is, indeed, not too difficult – though it is painfully slow and requires patience and maturity. Look at the deficiencies identified in the "realization" phase about your behavior and try to mend them systematically, one by one. Here are some simple guidelines:

- Speak less and in small segments – give others a chance to speak. Try utilizing the "split-second-silence" strategy that I outlined in chapter 25, that is: as and when you get an urge to speak – stop – give a pause – think – and now you would speak with greater maturity and less aggressiveness.
- Check to see how often you interrupt somebody while they are speaking, and control that.
- When you are listening to others, check consciously to see if

you are truly listening or if you are simply busy thinking of what you have to say when the other is finished.

- Keep a continuous check on your body gestures, body movements, and tone of speech. Control those actions because they are physical indicators of aggressiveness.
- Check to see if you are pressing your own beliefs and opinions too strongly. Also check to see if you have the tendency of repeating the same old tales and stories that you have recited hundreds of times before – control those urges.
- Check to see how you accept other people's opinions and thoughts.
- The last word: aggressiveness is bad in relationships. It is the anti-thesis of mutual respect. If everybody behaves aggressively, then how can a relationship function? Try to imagine how others would feel if you were too pushy, and at the same time, think of how you would feel if others were pushy with you. By doing this, you will appreciate both sides of feelings, and you will try to inculcate humbleness and a sense of mutual respect. Treat others as you want to be treated.

27
THE NEW RECONCILIATION

"A relationship is a compromise, not a competition."

Now, in this final frontier of resolution, we are moving into the twilight zone of relationship harmony and peace, and I would like to present a rather formal overview to the new reconciliation process. This process would be most useful if you have diligently gone through all the steps of the new perspectives presented in the book. To accentuate the uniqueness of the new approach, I would begin with a comparative analysis of the two processes – the current and the new. And to facilitate the explanation, I would consider, wherever needed, the scenario of the relationship of you and your spouse.

The Current Process

The sequential steps in the current reconciliation process are: the couple gets together, one-on-one with the mediator or counsellor; discusses what each said or did that caused the conflict; accepts fault; says sorry; agrees that it won't happen again; goes home to live happily ever after. The process ends here, with the hope that the reconciliation is complete, final, and permanent. Unfortunately, that doesn't happen because the process focuses only on correcting the inert entities of behavior, that is, what the couple said to each other that caused dissensions. It did not amend the person who generates those unwanted entities. A week or so goes by – and voila! – another confrontation occurs, and the couple says things to each other, perhaps different than the ones they said before, and another fight ensues. The relationship goes into spasm again, and there is a need for another reconciliation session. We go through the process again – we reconcile again – and once again go home happily. Not so, I am afraid – another week goes by – there is another confrontation of dissent. Like this, the story continues – and the process never ends. All of this happens simply because the focus of attention of the process is only on correcting the behavior and not the person who generates that behavior – and, therefore, it remains temporary and repetitive.

The New Process

The new process initially follows the same steps as the current process – of getting together and reconciling, but unlike the current process, it doesn't stop with the reconciliation of the entities. The process goes further into deeper levels of understanding – the inner personality – to find out why the disagreements occurred in the first place and why they happen so frequently. A total personality evaluation is carried out of all personality factors that impede the process of harmony. The aim is to look for the hidden anger and antagonism that may be causing negativity in the process.

Also, the new process puts greater emphasis on the reconciliation of the "self" first, before you begin the reconciliation with the other. The basic philosophy of the new process is that reconciliation is a matter between two selves – you and your spouse. Each self has to appropriately prepare itself for the process. In addition, these two selves have to lend their support to the mentors, so that the mentors can evaluate the source of anger and dissent that is housed deep down inside of you, which may be exerting sizable influence on your behavior.

Reconciliation with the Self

This process involves two things: reconciliation with the self; and generation of a reconciliation mindset. The question is: why do you need to reconcile with the self? Well! Your own self is a self like any other self, and a relationship is a matter between the two selves – and unless each self is ready, willing, and prepared for compromise, the reconciliation process cannot be successful. So what you need to do is ask yourself if you are at peace with yourself, and if you are ready for compromise – for if you are not at peace with your own self, chances are that you would not be at peace with the other, and any reconciliation effort would either be temporary in its impact or would go waste. In light of these conjectures, I would now present a few guidelines on preparing a reconciliation mindset.

- Firstly, you need to understand, accept, and resolve any unresolved issues of your own, for if you don't, they would generate anger and hostility inside you, and you may have the tendency to project your own anger onto the other during the course of reconciliation with the other.
- You have to let go of your built-up mental-tape of antagonistic feelings against the other, or at least, not utilize those pent-up feelings and perceptions as the basis of your judgment of the other's intentions. You have to give the reconciliation process an independent and unbiased chance to flourish.
- You have to generate a sense of empathy and respect for the feelings and opinions of the other.
- You have to humble your ego down, so that it doesn't interfere when you begin to accept compromises during the reconciliation process.
- You have to give up that strong conviction you hold of self-righteousness – that you are always right – and the only one who is right. Remember, the other person can also be equally right, if not more. Think of it this way – if you think you are right, and the other thinks he is right, then who is to decide who is really right? You have to put two different "rights" into one single "together right".
- You have to inculcate the strength to accept your own faults.

In short, you have to create a passion and a desire for reconciliation in order to achieve lasting relationship happiness. For the reconciliation process is merely a process, a means to reduce that undesirable distance between you two. It is not a process of uncovering your feelings of guilt, or of unravelling and exhibiting your weaknesses, nor is it a process of humiliating you, or letting you down – it's not a game of winning and losing – it is a game of winning and winning.

Exercise: Checking Your Emotional Thermostat

Since it is essential to have an emotionally stable mindset before you go into the reconciliation process, I have an interesting exercise for you to check your emotional thermostat. Here is an easy way to do it:

- Sit comfortably on a chair.
- Join both hands together – softly – palms holding and snuggling each other.

- Close your eyes, and blank your mind of any thoughts.
- Focus your eyes and mind on the inside of your body.
- Now, feel the vibrations flowing through and crossing over the two hands, and also throughout your body. Sense these currents and vibrations – and see if they are: "warm, relaxed, positive" – or "agitated, tense, negative".

A good exercise – you can do it alone, or it may be better to do it with a friend or your spouse. You would need some practice before you can realize its true value. I use this exercise quite often – by myself, as well as with friends. By simply holding the hands of a person, softly, in my hands – I can sense the vibrations and find out the state of positivity, negativity, or relaxedness of the other person.

The Re-Making Process

There are two facets of reconciliation:
- Continuous reconciliation
- Ad-hoc reconciliation

Continuous reconciliation is a preferred method of choice – you don't wait until the anger has reached a boiling point – you communicate on a continuous basis to clarify and ameliorate the discord. Reconciliation should be as often and as frequent as the discord. You can't fight with each other everyday, but reconcile only once a week. Continuous reconciliation would stop the build-up of the mental tape of anger and discontentment.

Ad-hoc reconciliation means carrying out the process only when the situation has reached the breaking point. This is the most commonly used practice – though not the most suitable one – but perhaps the only recourse available to you. Depending on the severity of the situation, there are three options for reconciliation:
- Option 1: Direct discussions between the two persons
- Option 2: Intervention by a relative or a friend
- Option 3: Formal intervention and mediation by a counsellor or a psychologist

Option One: Direct Discussions

This is the most plausible and intelligent option, because you two are the only ones who know the real story of what went wrong and why. This is the only option that lends itself to "continuous reconciliation". If you can get into the habit of opening up to each other, directly and as often as required, you can easily achieve that permanent sense of harmony in your relationship.

Options Two and Three: Intervention by a Friend or Relative – or by a Counsellor or Psychologist

The process for both of these options is similar, except that Option 3 is a bit more formal. These are the only options available to you if you think you are too emotionally charged-up and bruised, and you can't handle the process by yourself. There are a few important aspects of these options that you should keep in mind:

- It's your problem and not that of the intervener – so you have to be a full and willing participant in the process. The external help acts only as an instigating catalyst, it can't do things for you. You yourself have to have that inside willingness and determination to make the process succeed. To join together in "holy reconciliation", you have to once more say "I do" – as you did at the time of your marriage vows – though, this time, you have to say "I do" – with my "heart", as well as my "personality".

- You must watch carefully to see that the reconciliation doesn't ultimately lead to even more anger or hurt feelings than what you started with. Also, the presence of a third person should not give you the feeling of let-down, of shame and defeat and impart that feeling that you have lost your self-respect. For if that happens – it can generate more anger inside you, and make the process futile.

The Process

Finally, a few guidelines, for the mentors, on the functioning of the new process:

- The mediator or the counsellor would begin the process as usual, by discussing what you said to each other that caused the discord.

- Once that is cleared up, the counsellor should attempt to identify if every confrontation is caused by the same factors that caused the most recent discord.

- Find out the pattern of discordant behavior.

- Identify the factors – personality or otherwise – that are responsible for this repetitive confrontation of disagreement.
- Establish a profile of those personality characteristics.
- Go deep down to the source of those feelings that cause the disagreements.
- Discuss with you two those inner feelings of anger and discord.
- Bring about an understanding of how permanent harmony can be achieved.
- Bring about an understanding of compromise by actuating source-level changes and amendments to your personality.

28
HUMBLE SURRENDERS

"Forgiveness is not only a gift for the others;
It elevates your own ego also."

This is the last chapter of my mainframe discussion of the dilemma of makings and breakings of relationships. To bring my discussion to a close in an aura of modesty and humbleness, I saved two very appealing ideas for this last chapter. The aim is to impress upon you that a relationship is a very gentle, soft, and sensitive issue, and therefore, it should be treated with utmost care and love. The two topics of discussion in this chapter are: Forgiveness, and Humble Surrenders.

Forgiveness

- Your mother-in-law has ill-treated you.
- Your spouse has mistreated you.
- Your brother has inflicted emotional pain on you.
- Your friend has betrayed you, etc., etc.

You are hurt – you are angry – you are full of hatred for all those who you think have done wrong to you, and have emotionally hurt you. Tit for tat – you want to retaliate – you want to take revenge – you want to punish those people – you want to teach them a lesson. In fact, you are already doing so – retaliating – taking revenge, in one form or another. You are constantly ill-treating them – sometimes openly – most of the times diplomatically – and almost all the time mentally. You cannot forget – you cannot forgive – or you don't want to forgive.

Sound familiar? Then let me stop you here for a minute and ask you a simple question: "who do you really think you are hurting"? Nobody but your own "self". Staying constantly hyped-up in that state of anger, hatred, and revenge – mentally or physically – keeps your stress hormones at high levels all the time, and your anger-vengeance-filled state of mind is eating away your inside – your inner peace and happiness – slowly, systematically, and silently. You are thinking that you are inflicting pain on those who have done wrong to you – not so – you are really inflicting pain on yourself – nameless and unseen pain. And in this state, your anger-filled ego is so wrapped-up in the feeling of revenge that your inner wisdom is completely blinded – you don't know what you are doing – you cannot differentiate between right and wrong – all you think is that the other is wrong – and that you are right. And in the process of doing so, you are not only hurting your own self, but you are also hurting the others. You are, unknowingly, leading your relationship towards permanent disharmony. As long as you keep hoarding the hidden feelings of anger and hatred inside you, you will never be able to reconcile and be at peace with others – or even with your own self.

What can you do? Let me start with forgetting. Forget it. You will never ever be able to forget – not as long as you live. Emotionally-charged entities go permanently on your "mental-tape", and they become a non-erasable part of your memory. What about "forgiving" – yes – that's possible – but it depends on your will to do so.

Why should you forgive? Well – good question – but here are some realistic scenarios to think about:

- How long are you going to carry this unwanted baggage of anger, hatred, and revenge? If you are young – you still have plenty to live – are you going to carry this dangerous cargo for as long as you live? If you are old, then what worth is it to waste the few years that you have left of your life with this grudge?
- You are not perfect either – nobody is perfect – surely you must have also made many blunders in life – and surely people have forgiven you – and you have forgiven your self also – then why can't you forgive others.
- Perhaps the people that you hate are not at fault – they never said or did anything bad to you – it is simply your own faulty interpretation of what they did that is causing anger in you.
- Even God forgives everybody – including you – then how come you can't forgive others.

Remember! Forgiveness is divine – it's a very powerful force – when you forgive others – you also forgive your own self in the process – it is immensely satisfying. It is the most beautiful act of life. Bring in that divine sense of humbleness in you, and make an honest attempt to forgive the others. Don't just say that you forgive – mean it also – empty your mind of the feeling of anger and hatred. Do it honestly – and with the bigness of your heart. Forgiveness is an extremely difficult act – and very few people really have the strength to do it. Most people would just say, for the sake of saying only, that they have forgiven, but deep down within their hearts, they keep upholding the grudge – the anger – the hatred. They really "never" forgive. Forgiveness is very powerful – very satisfying – so much so that your own ego will feel good about it – so at least forgive others for the sake of your own ego, if not for somebody else's sake.

Humble Surrenders

This is my simple new creation, by which I mean – a laid-back frame of mind – a humble and gentle behavioral attitude towards relationship confrontations and annoyances. It is a very stress-free way of dealing with relationship problems – you are always mellow and at peace with yourself. It reinforces you with a strong sense of maturity and serenity. In addition, this attitude also helps to disarm the other person, thus making him/her humble and serene also, which makes it easy to establish positive communication with the person.

As you know, in day-to-day life and living, there are many chores of life that are essential to be performed. It is in the performance of these chores that relationship confrontations and minor and major annoyances ensue. If you don't handle these discords amicably, they can lead your relationship towards disharmony. The chores of life are generally achievable by two means:

- Confrontational – demanding
- Humbleness – requesting

The first approach leads to ego-awakening – anger – antagonism – and a build-up of bad feelings. The second approach accomplishes the same task through mutual humbleness and help. The goal of the two approaches is, indeed, the same – to accomplish a task – except that the first approach achieves the goal with anger and the second one with love and understanding. Surely, therefore, it makes good sense to use a more humble approach to achieving goals.

There is a simple method that I have developed vis-à-vis the "Humble Surrenders" that I find very effective in handling confrontational scenarios arising out of the performance of day-to-day chores of life and living – without creating a full blown relationship brawl. I call it the "Reverse Psychology" method. I have already outlined it in an earlier chapter, but I would like to repeat it. Reverse Psychology is, of course, not an academic or literary term – it is just a nomenclature I have coined to explain a concept that is very useful in relationship situations. Let me now explain the concept of "Reverse Psychology" – and it would be easier to understand it through an example.

Let's consider the scenario: your husband has just come back from the office, opens up a can of beer, goes to the sofa, and sits down to watch his favourite hockey game on the television. You would, instead, like him to first take the garbage out – almost right away – because it is making a mess in the house. So here we have a confrontational scenario that we want to resolve amicably.

The first thing to do, for all such situations, is to define the goal. The goal in this case is: "garbage to go out", almost immediately. There are two options that you can exercise:

- One, to shout at your spouse – get angry – and demand that he take the garbage out – now – right away, rather than drinking his beer and watching his game.
- The other is to request him to take the garbage out.

With the first option, he may do the task, but it certainly involves the remote possibility that he would get mad at your naggings. And if you have used demanding strategies before, his mental tape would be full of anger-filled feelings about your daily naggings. The harmony of the relationship can certainly run the risk of being damaged.

With the second option, he may procrastinate, and say that he would take the garbage out after a while, when his game is finished – which for you may be very late in the evening, and you would want to get the garbage out – now – now.

Here is my method of "Reverse Psychology" that you can utilize with the second approach – that of "requesting".

This is what you should say to your husband: "Honey – the garbage needs to be taken out – but it looks like you are tired now, and you are watching your game – why don't you relax – I will take the garbage out myself". In all probability, I think he would jump from his seat at once and take the garbage out first. So what is the end result – the goal is accomplished – the garbage has gone out – and that's what you wanted.

This is the power of a humble request under the guise of what I call the "Reverse Psychology" approach.

Now I am sure that this seems like a silly little example, but it is good enough to make a point. The point is that a relationship is far above the petty annoyances or chores of life – a relationship is a matter of love, respect, and care – you can't sacrifice a good relationship at the altar of petty and meaningless chores of life and living. You need to handle those chores with love, humbleness, mutual help, and care. You don't have to demand and confront a bad situation when the situation can be resolved through a humble request – for, after all, look at what the aim is, and if the aim is being achieved by humble surrenders – why not exercise that option.

In closing, all I can say is that "humble surrenders" is a beautiful phenomenon – just try it and see how calm and serene you would feel. Humble surrenders doesn't, in any way, mean a let-down or defeat for your ego, or a loss of self-respect – it is simply a gesture that indicates how much you care for the people you love. It manifests a genuine desire and willingness on your part to bend backwards and drop your ego-arrogance guards down for the sake of finding relationship happiness. The wisdom of humble surrenders constitutes the following principles:

- You throw away your ego-arrogance for the moment – mellow down your aggressiveness – and exercise high level of maturity.
- You manifest an attitude of requesting, rather than one of demanding during your confrontations.
- You avoid a direct challenge or a direct hurt to the other person's ego.
- You don't try to put blame only on the other – you try to find out if you are wrong too.
- By being humble yourself, you can humble the other's psyche also, and this would help resolve your differences through mutual understanding, rather than through a fight.

29
PEARLS OF WISDOM
- THE LESSONS LEARNT

"A relationship is like a delicate thin thread;
Once broken — you can tie a knot —
But there will always be a knot."

This chapter is simply a synopsis of the main principles that you have learnt from the new ideas presented in this book. They are included here to remind you of things you can or cannot do in relationships. You should draw up a list of the most important behavioral modalities and continuously practice in your daily interactions, to ensure long-lasting harmony in your relationships.

Thoughts for Relationship Harmony

1. Firstly, you must continuously assert with yourself that you do have a genuine desire to have a happy and healthy relationship at all times — and manifest your honest commitment to this goal.

2. Next, you must remember that a relationship is a matter that involves two people, each with their own unique profile — a framework of feelings, emotions, thinking, and personality. And the relationship will only function when there is equality and mutual respect for each other's convictions.

3. Treat the other as you treat your own self, or as you would like others to treat you.

4. Everybody is different in every respect — likings-dislikings, rights-wrongs, behavior-attitude — so don't try to change others and don't expect others to submit to your way of behaving. Create consensus out of diversity.

5. Stop thinking that you are the only one who is the smartest of all. Others think the same way too, and others may be even smarter than you.

6. Stop being outward-directed – to see the faults of others only, but never your own. Look inside and try to find your own faults also. You are as perfect or imperfect as anybody else.

7. Stop giving advice just because you think you know better than the other. Give advice only when asked for, and also learn to accept when others give you advice.

8. Don't carry out relationship interactions in the mode of blaming others – accept an equal share of the responsibility for the demise of the relationship.

9. When asking for something, make a request, not a demand.

10. Don't carry out your relationships on the basis of your preconceived impressions about the other. Give the relationship an independent chance to grow.

11. If you are insistently aggressive, nobody is going to tolerate that and have a relationship with you. How would you feel if others were aggressive with you also? Relationships cannot continue and survive if each party continues to impose his own pushiness onto the other.

12. If you have a big ego, so does the other – perhaps even bigger than yours. Egos are never accommodating – so stop challenging the other's ego.

13. Reconciliation is not a tool for fighting; it is a means of compromising.

14. Don't hoard anger inside you, for the other person – it will never let you maintain a genuinely clean and happy relationship.

Before You Break...

1. Give your relationship and love another chance to reunite
2. Humble your ego
3. Break the silence
4. Reach out and connect
5. Surrender your self
6. Show your genuine desire to ameliorate
7. Openly and honestly discuss your feelings

8. Don't complain or fight – discuss
9. Accept the possibility that you can be wrong also
10. Accept your faults - gracefully
11. Say sorry for the misunderstanding
12. Show your true love and respect

Reconciliation Commandments

1. Look for suitable moment to break the silence – to connect.
2. Reach out and touch – sit down peacefully – hold each other's hands.
3. Start with a single, non-challenging, non-threatening issue.
4. Discuss one issue at a time.
5. Humbly surrender yourself.
6. Don't open the discussion by blaming the other.
7. Open your mind to all possibilities.
8. Tell your feelings honestly and as soon as possible.
9. Deal with the current – don't bring in the past.
10. Try to look for a middle ground in arguments.
11. Make the discussion a matter of two loving hearts, rather than a fight of two egos.
12. Avoid emotional outbursts.
13. Don't bring anger into the discussion.
14. Don't be judgmental.
15. Don't fight – discuss.
16. Be sensitive to each other's feelings and viewpoints.
17. Be respectful.
18. Have the courage to accept your fault.
19. Say sorry if you need to.
20. Agree to forgive and forget
21. Agree that you would not let little annoyances damage your beautiful relationship.
22. Close the discussion with affectionate partings.

Pearls of Wisdom

- Worship togetherness – live in a single marriage – not two individual marriages – his and hers.
- Behave with others the same way you would like others to behave with you.

- Keep a clean and transparent mind.
- Tell your feelings honestly and as soon as possible – before the feelings have a chance to accumulate.
- Others' feelings are as important as yours – be compassionate and tolerant.
- Listen more – talk less.
- Be 100% honest – 100% of the time.
- Accept yourself as well as others – as is.
- If you love somebody – then why change what you love.
- Live in the present – there is no ego in the present to interfere with your thinking.
- Share your feelings with each other on a daily basis.
- A relationship is beautiful if it is based on love rather than need.
- Nurture love.

The Essentials of Togetherness

- At least once a day – if not more – affectionately touch and hold each other.
- At least twice a week – if not more – say the unsaid words: "I love you".
- Find occasions or tasks for which you can praise and compliment each other.
- Bring flowers – flowers are not only meant for birthdays or anniversaries – flowers are for love.
- At least once in two weeks – go out for a dinner and a movie.
- At least once a week – make the evening dinner and the atmosphere more uniquely romantic.
- Volunteer for a greater responsibility and share of the household chores.
- Find ways to regularly check each other's happiness thermostat.
- Find a moment when you can say to each other: "life would have been meaningless without you".
- And the final test of love – say that: "if I have nine more lives – I will ask for only your love for each life".

A Thought That Changed My Life

"Thoughts are thoughts – they have their own mind – they come when they come".

I am reminded of a thought that I want to share with you – a thought that virtually changed my life – perhaps it may change your life too.

I have attended the funerals of many of my friends and relatives before – but this one that I attended recently, of a dear friend who died rather prematurely, deeply touched my heart. A large gathering of relatives and friends was present at the crematorium. Before the actual cremation ceremony, there were several speeches about the life and accomplishments of the departing soul. Many good things were being said about the person – how he led his life – what he did for himself– but, more specifically, "what he did for others". I was sitting with my head down – sad – sombre – somnolent – with tears in my eyes – listening to what was being said. Suddenly, a thought flashed in my head – "what would people say about me when I die"?

That's it – that's the thought?

But, that thought struck me like a bolt of lightning from the sky. A total blankness spread over my mind. I asked myself: what have I done for others for which they will remember me – and no viable answer came out of my mind. There was nothing that I could be proud of. I felt an emptiness – a vacuum – an emotional pain in my heart – pain that no medical science could diagnose or cure.

Sure! I could console myself by arguing that – how does it all matter to my friend now – how does he know or care about what is being said about him – he is dead and gone anyway. But I guess that is neither the question nor the answer – it is simply a shameful excuse in our defence.

Think of it this way – we get one trip through life – most of that we spend doing things for ourselves. Everyone does for oneself anyway – what matters is what we do for others – without conditions – without expectations – with pure and genuine love. Giving is doubly more pleasurable than receiving – the more you give of yourself, the more that will come flowing back to you.

"Leaving some memorable footprints – something to think about."

Yes! It did, indeed, change my life in many simple ways – but through many simple "humble surrenders".

THE EPILOGUE

Beyond the senses are their objects;
Beyond the objects is the mind;
Beyond the mind is pure reason;
Beyond reason is the great "self".

The wise should restrain speech in mind;
Mind in the knowing Self;
The knowing Self in the great Self;
The great Self in the Self of Peace.

The Upanishads

EPILOGUE
A BOUQUET OF ROSES FOR MY CHILDREN

"If you dwell on the past, you will waste the present;
If you ignore the past, you will miss the future."

Time passes by – it waits for nobody. A lot of time has passed by my side. I have lived for many more years than you have, and have bruised my body and mind over these years, in order to learn about life. Now, at this stage, when I look back and remember things I did or did not do, I say to myself: "I wish I had known then what I know "now"" – or perhaps more appropriately – I wish someone could have told me then what I now know "myself" – I could have, perhaps, avoided some unnecessary bumps and bruises along the way to arrive at where I am today. Although my life has turned out to be pretty satisfying, it could have been more so had I known a few things, and known them "earlier".

In an attempt to spare you some of the bumps and bruises, I have prepared a bouquet of roses for you – to share with you some thoughts that you may wish to incorporate "now" as part of your lives – to achieve happiness, prosperity, and aesthetic oneness of body, mind, and soul.

I know advice is easy to come by, and you young people are virtually buried under it. I am sure, by now, you must have mastered the art of avoiding listening, while still giving the impression that you are paying attention. I guess we all do that. In any case, my intentions are simply to make sure that after umpteen number of years, you don't have to say like I do now – that: "I wish someone had told me then what I now know myself", or "I could have done better had I known a few things and known them earlier."

Here are some pearls of wisdom that I have collected over these number of years – a few guiding principles for a beautiful and simple life. Think about them each day, and you will begin to feel the serenity, simplicity, and fullness of life.

1. Be Happy

You get only one trip through life – you can lead it happily or unhappily – you can enjoy it or waste it – the choice is exclusively yours and yours alone to make.

Happiness is not a happening – it's a realization – it's a state of mind – something inside you that can be realized by you and you alone. Happiness is not something lying in wait on the street corner – which you can grab and own – it is the creation of your mind alone. You can be happy and fulfilled in almost anything little you have, or you may be unhappy even if you have everything that you ever wanted to have.

Happiness is not something that happens or doesn't happen – it's there all the time. What is important is not the moment-by-moment, or task-by-task happiness, but the total continuous natural-state-of-mind-happiness that is of value. Being and having are two different things. Having cannot accentuate being, but being can overrule having. Life based on having rather than being is virtually meaningless – at least on the higher levels of intellectual and spiritual platforms – and that is the platform of happiness. So what are you waiting for – grab hold of life – enjoy the trip – and leave some memorable footprints. Remember the sayings of the Indian hermit, "Kabir":

**"When you were born, you were crying and the world was smiling.
Lead your life in such a way – that when you die –
you would be smiling, and the world would be crying."**

Kabir

Greet each day with a smile – the day will greet you back in the same way. The world is nothing but a mirror image of your own thinking – it's happy if you are happy – it's miserable if you are miserable.

2. Know Yourself

The most essential elements of your life include the following, as a minimum:

- To know your self, and to know others in relation to your self
- To accept your self as you are, and to accept others as they are.

Ownership and knowledge of the self is the most beautiful thing. If you don't know your own self – who you are – what you are – why you do what you do – then your own unique existence is meaningless. Unfortunately, a large majority of us don't know our selves. If you don't know others, then you would always be projecting your own self onto others, and you would want others to do what you think is right – whether that right is right or not. This is what creates relationship conflicts.

In addition to knowing yourself and others – you have to accept yourself as you are – and accept others as they are. If you don't accept yourself – there will be an unending internal conflict inside you. If you don't accept others as they are – there will be two conflicts – internal, as well as external. This is because acceptance and conflict have a cause-effect relationship. Conflict is the outcome of non-acceptance. On the other end, compassion is the outcome of acceptance.

Acceptance is easier when you are yourself. Be yourself – whatever you are – and let people accept you the way you are. Most people try to be what they are not – they try to be what somebody else is – they try to imitate and steal faces and personalities because they are empty in themselves – and they seemingly get a feeling of fulfillment by being somebody else. What a weird paradox – when somebody steals something – we call him a thief – and we punish him. But when somebody steals a persona – a personality – we praise him.

If you get into the habit of wearing masks – personas – different faces than your own – you would need so many masks. In fact, in one 24-hour day, you would need to change your mask almost as many times as you get into a new situation – it's one mask when you go to work – it's another when you come home – it's a different persona when you go to church – it's a different personality when you speak to a friend, a relative, or your spouse. If you do that, you will lose the most precious possession of all – "trust" – people just won't know who and what you really are, and they won't trust you. So be what you are – and be one with yourself – inside and outside.

3.   Live in the Present

Be like the flowers – they only live in the present – not the past – not the future – and they share their fragrance without any expectations of any returns. Present is reality – past is repentance – and future is desires.

Past and future are vicious circles, they wrap around you and never let you enjoy the moment at hand. And the moment at hand keeps moving – it never waits for anyone – the moment of the present either becomes the past or it becomes the future – it's never stationary – that's how transitory the present is. So if you don't enjoy the present – you will miss the past as well as the future.

And living in the present also helps you to be focused – for then all of your energies are single-focused – and that helps you concentrate and enjoy and achieve the task at hand much more easily and effectively. Living in the present also safeguards you from the damaging influences of your ego – because the ego is either past or future. Ego is accumulation – ego is memory – ego interferes with your present and influences your future.

4.   Have Faith

Have faith in yourself – in others – and in God. Faith is the basis of all human endeavours – whatever its nature, size, or intensity. Every task or activity that you undertake is based on some type of faith.

The origin of faith is really God – because it is the starting point of our existence, and unless we have faith in our existence or in the natural order of things, nothing we do in life would have a stable platform. It's not possible to handle life and the world on your own. People will tell you that strength and wisdom come from within yourself, but they are not being honest. Yes, it does come from within, but only because you have faith in yourself – in your existence – and in God. God provides the steady foundation of your life. He is always there – always the same. Our trust in God teaches us the meaning of the word "faith".

5.   Worship Togetherness

Marriage is a cooperative endeavour, not an individualistic competitive sport. Two-getherness is not two people doing two things separately, but two people doing one thing together. Strengthen your relationship each day with love, care and support.

The ultimate basis of a relationship is trust. A relationship based on mutual trust, honesty, respect, and tolerance is infinitely satisfying. Be each other's best friend.

6. Love Life

The genesis of relationship is eulogized in love. Love is everywhere and plentiful. Love is singularly the most important and most beautiful facet of life – nothing else in life comes even close to it in comparison. Love is the only thing that reminds you that you are more than the body – you are the mind.

When you become one in love – giving and taking becomes the same. The love that you experience in giving is far above the love that you experience in receiving. Love is a three-pronged emotion:

- Love for life
- Love for yourself
- Love for others

Firstly, and most importantly – you must love life – for if you don't love life, you won't love anything around life – and it is an existence of hopelessness and negativity. Next, you must love yourself – as you are. For if you don't love and accept yourself, there is very little chance that you would love and accept anybody else. If you can inflict pain on your own self, you would have no hesitation in inflicting pain on others.

To love yourself seems funny – because to love, you need someone else. But the concept is that by loving yourself, you will learn how to love – and therefore, you will learn how to love others. So love for yourself – in fact – teaches you love for others.

Lastly, you must love others for what they are. If you love somebody, then why try to change what you love. In fact, love for others is essential for your own balanced life. The more you give of yourself, the more will come flowing back to you. You will feel good about yourself.

7. Be Positive

Positivity exudes positivity. Wear a positive persona all the time and you would exuberate a positive aura and positive vibrations all around you. People will experience a feeling of pleasantness and aesthetic tranquility when they enter your magnetic field of positivity. You will see things as they are – more positively. Negativity breeds repulsion and unpleasantness.

Positivity accentuates relationship harmony. Contrary to scientific rules, in relationships, two positives are always better and closer than either two negatives or one positive and one negative.

I must recount this beautiful scenario, which I found to exuberate the power of positivity and togetherness. A couple that I know was going through financial hardships, and when I spoke about this issue, their answer was as follows:

> **We have desires and commitment.**
> **We have power and ability.**
> **We have dreams and will.**
> **We have hope and faith.**
> **We have passion and confidence.**
> **We have love and togetherness.**
> **We have each other – you and me.**

8. Be Honest

Honesty is an important life attribute, both for you and for the other. Honesty indicates that you are the same – inside and outside – and people will trust you. You will exuberate confidence, and you are not afraid of anything – because you are honest. Honesty with others means that your relationship with them is one of openness.

Honesty is important for your own self also. In fact, honesty starts with being honest with you. For if you are not honest with yourself, you can hardly be honest with anybody else. If you can cheat yourself – surely you would have no remorse in cheating others.

The highest form of accountability is always to the self. You have to be accountable to yourself – more than to others. The highest form of disgrace comes when you have fallen in your own eyes. Honesty will give you the strength to say what you want to say, and people would not derive any wrong meanings from what you say.

Shrewdness – another name for cunningness, at least in the context of relationships – is the antithesis of honesty. A cunning person is generally not very honest or straightforward, and because he is cunning, he thinks everybody else is cunning. So when you say something to him, he would always misconstrue and misinterpret the meaning and context of your behavior, because he himself is cunning. A relationship with a person like this is virtually untenable, because he is not the same inside as he is outside – he is not honest and transparent. Honesty gives you a spiritual sense of elegance, inner confidence, and inner happiness – your wisdom is at its best.

9. Be Compassionate

Compassion makes you a person – it makes you human. Compassion is a matter of the heart – it makes you feel for others as you will feel for yourself – or as you would like others to feel for you. Typically, our misery emanates from two situations:

- We don't receive love, or
- We don't give love.

Both situations would teach you an important lesson. If you don't receive love and you feel bad about it, then think of how bad others must be feeling for not receiving love from you – which should tell you to share your love and compassion with others. If you don't give love, then how can you expect others to give love to you?

Compassion and love are closely intertwined – you love because you have compassion – and you have compassion because you love. If you have no compassion, then probably, you have no love. And because compassion is a matter of the mind and heart, it is the purest form of love. Compassion involves your highest and purest form of energy and love.

Compassion and expectation are antitheses of each other – when you have compassion, there are no expectations of anything in return. And if you have expectations, then there is no compassion. Compassion is a realization, not a need. Be compassionate – it would provide you with infinite spiritual fullness and serenity.

10. Simplify Life

Simplicity is the key to freedom and fulfillment.

Many of us believe that a good life and freedom are impossible without affluence, cutthroat competition, and conflict. The cultivation and expansion of needs is the antithesis of wisdom. Life based on "having" rather than "doing" or "being" breeds boredom, ennui, and a sense of isolation and soul-weariness. Free yourself from the "ifs", "buts", and "musts" of life. Follow the natural order of things – and simplicity and happiness will automatically unfold themselves to you.

May God be with you – always?

ABOUT THE AUTHOR

Subhash Puri is an international speaker, lecturer, and consultant. For the past 30 years, he has taught in various universities, delivered numerous public lectures and seminars, and undertaken consultations in various countries around the world, in Business/Quality Management and Human Motivation. He has published numerous papers and fourteen textbooks, including translations in several languages.

A large proportion of his time has also been spent in understanding and researching many facets of human behavior – and, on a personal level, he has been instrumental in guiding and mentoring people in the area of human relationships. This book is the outcome of that passion and experiential diligence.

He and his family make their home in Ontario, Canada.

For consultations, Mr. Puri can be reached through his email: scpuri@rogers.com.

166356

Made in the USA